DK Pocket Genius

SHARKS

FACTS AT YOUR FINGERTIPS

D0287563

LONDON, NEW YORK, MUNICH,
MELBOURNE, and DELHI

DK INDIA
Project editor Virien Chopra
Project art editor Nishesh Batnagar
Senior editor Kingshuk Ghoshal
Senior art editor Govind Mittal
Editors Rashmi Rajan, Jubbi Francis
Assistant art editor Tanya Mehrotra
DTP designers Dheeraj Arora, Jaypal Singh
Picture researcher Sumedha Chopra
Managing editor Saloni Talwar
Managing art editor Romi Chakraborty
CTS manager Balwant Singh
Production manager Pankaj Sharma

DK LONDON
Senior editor Fleur Star
Senior art editor Philip Letsu
US editor Margaret Parrish
Jacket editor Manisha Majithia
Jacket designer Laura Brim
Jacket design development manager
Sophia Tampakopolous
Production editor Ben Marcus
Production controller Mary Slater

Publisher Andrew Macintyre
Associate publishing director Liz Wheeler
Art director Phil Ormerod
Publishing director Jonathan Metcalf

Consultant Dr. Trevor Day

First published in the United States in 2012
by DK Publishing
345 Hudson Street, New York, New York 10014
Copyright © 2012 Dorling Kindersley Limited
15 16 10 9 8 7 6 5
012–184272–Jun/12

A catalog record for this book
is available from the Library of Congress.
ISBN: 978-0-7566-9286-5

Printed and bound by South China
Printing Company, China

**Discover more at
www.dk.com**

CONTENTS

Scales and sizes
This book contains profiles of sharks, rays, skates, and chimaeras with scale drawings to indicate their size.

6 ft (1.8 m)   8 in (20 cm)

Endangered sharks
This label indicates that the fish is endangered or critically endangered.

ENDANGERED

The shark

Sharks are cartilaginous fish, meaning they have a skeleton made of cartilage, a lighter and more flexible substance than bone. Millions of years of evolution have made sharks some of the deadliest predators in the oceans. Excellent eyesight, powerful jaws, and a streamlined body make them efficient and dominant hunters.

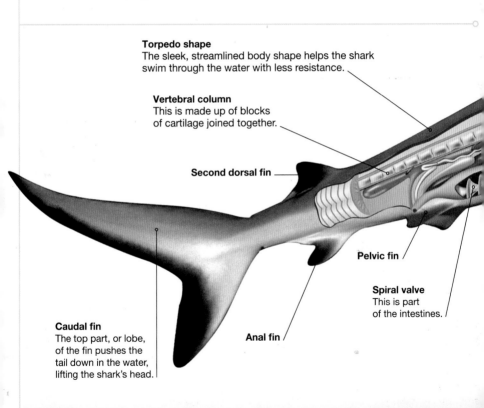

Torpedo shape
The sleek, streamlined body shape helps the shark swim through the water with less resistance.

Vertebral column
This is made up of blocks of cartilage joined together.

Second dorsal fin

Pelvic fin

Spiral valve
This is part of the intestines.

Caudal fin
The top part, or lobe, of the fin pushes the tail down in the water, lifting the shark's head.

Anal fin

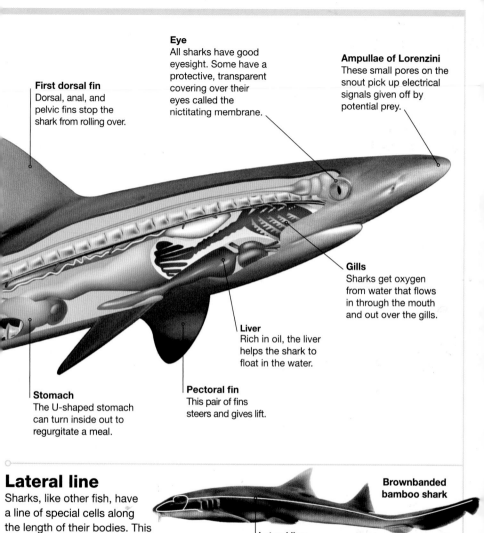

First dorsal fin
Dorsal, anal, and pelvic fins stop the shark from rolling over.

Eye
All sharks have good eyesight. Some have a protective, transparent covering over their eyes called the nictitating membrane.

Ampullae of Lorenzini
These small pores on the snout pick up electrical signals given off by potential prey.

Gills
Sharks get oxygen from water that flows in through the mouth and out over the gills.

Liver
Rich in oil, the liver helps the shark to float in the water.

Stomach
The U-shaped stomach can turn inside out to regurgitate a meal.

Pectoral fin
This pair of fins steers and gives lift.

Lateral line

Sharks, like other fish, have a line of special cells along the length of their bodies. This line detects vibrations in the water, such as the movements of potential prey.

Brownbanded bamboo shark

Lateral line
The white line on this image follows the actual lateral line of this shark.

Making sense

Sharks have superb senses that allow them to be among the top predators on the planet. Aside from the five senses they share with people—sight, touch, taste, hearing, and smell—sharks also have an electrical sense that helps them locate prey.

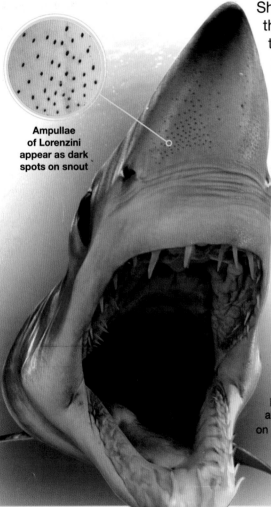

Ampullae of Lorenzini appear as dark spots on snout

Mako shark

Electrical sense

All living things give off electrical signals. Sharks have special organs called the ampullae of Lorenzini that detect such signals to help them find prey at close range. The ampullae are a network of thousands of pores on a shark's snout. The pores pick up the signals and transmit them to the shark's brain, helping it pinpoint the prey's location.

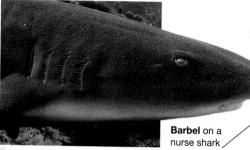

Barbels

Some sharks that live near the seabed have sensitive, whiskerlike organs called barbels that help them "taste" and "smell" chemicals given off by prey. Dragging the barbels over the seabed allows them to pick up vibrations in the sand made by buried sea animals.

Barbel on a nurse shark

Eye of a scalloped hammerhead shark

Seeing farther

Most sharks have good eyesight, and some can see well even in dim light. Hammerhead sharks have another advantage. Their eyes are set wide apart, giving them a large field of vision. This allows them to not only see farther, but also to see above and below at all times.

Nostril of a Port Jackson shark

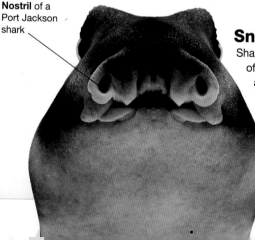

Sniffing out

Sharks have a highly developed sense of smell. Some species can detect a drop of blood in the water from hundreds of yards away. A shark can tell the direction of its prey as soon as one of its nostrils detects the scent, in the same way our ears tell us where sound is coming from.

Teeth and jaws

Shark teeth come in different shapes and sizes and have different uses. Long, curved teeth help to get hold of slippery fish, while serrated (sawlike) teeth are used to bite off chunks of prey. Some sharks have tiny teeth that strain food from the water, while others have flat teeth to crush hard-shelled prey.

Basking sharks can have up to 1,500 teeth

No chewing

Basking sharks and megamouth sharks are some of the largest sharks, but they fill up on the smallest prey—tiny creatures called plankton. These sharks are filter feeders, which means they use their teeth like a strainer to filter plankton from the water.

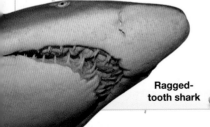

Ragged-tooth shark

Sharp as a needle

Sharks that feed on slippery fish and squid need to be able to hold on to their prey. The long, pointed teeth of these sharks grip the prey's body, preventing it from escaping.

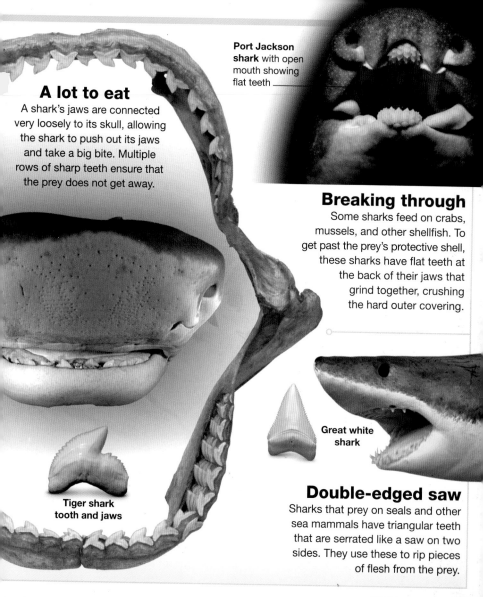

Port Jackson shark with open mouth showing flat teeth

A lot to eat

A shark's jaws are connected very loosely to its skull, allowing the shark to push out its jaws and take a big bite. Multiple rows of sharp teeth ensure that the prey does not get away.

Breaking through

Some sharks feed on crabs, mussels, and other shellfish. To get past the prey's protective shell, these sharks have flat teeth at the back of their jaws that grind together, crushing the hard outer covering.

Great white shark

Tiger shark tooth and jaws

Double-edged saw

Sharks that prey on seals and other sea mammals have triangular teeth that are serrated like a saw on two sides. They use these to rip pieces of flesh from the prey.

Swimming

Sharks are some of the fastest swimmers in the ocean. They propel themselves through water by moving their tails from side to side. Swimming not only helps a shark to catch prey, but also moves water over its gills, allowing it to breathe.

S is for swimming

As a shark swims, its body curves in an S-shape, pushing itself forward. It uses its pectoral fins to provide lift and change direction. It cannot flap its fins, but by making small changes to the angle of the fins, it can move up, down, left, and right.

1. Muscles in the body contract, making the head curve to one side.

Small-spotted catshark

2. The curve moves to the middle of the body as the head moves to the other side.

Step by step

Some sharks that live near coral reefs or on the seabed use their pectoral fins not only for swimming, but for walking as well. These sharks pull themselves along with their fins while they search the reef or seabed for food.

Epaulette shark

Swim or die

Sharks breathe by using their gills to draw oxygen from the water. Most sharks are able to pump water over their gills by swallowing water as they swim. However, some sharks, such as the mako shark, have lost this ability and must keep swimming so that water is continuously passing over their gills.

Gill slits open and close, letting out water

Shortfin mako shark

3. The curve ends at the tail, providing the shark with a speed boost.

Oxygen pump

Some sharks that live on the ocean floor do not move around much. To get oxygen, they take in water through two tubes called spiracles. Muscular movements draw in water through the spiracles, and pass it over the gills that are located on the underside of the body.

Spiracle located behind eye

Japanese angel shark

Reproduction

Sharks produce pups in three ways. Some lay eggs—they are oviparous. Some give birth to live young—they are viviparous. But most are both—they are ovoviviparous, which means the young develop inside eggs but hatch while they are still inside their mother.

Inside an egg

Oviparous sharks lay their eggs in the water, where they are in constant danger of being swept away. To prevent this, the eggs of some species, such as catsharks, have tendrils that wrap around seaweed, anchoring the eggs while the baby shark grows inside.

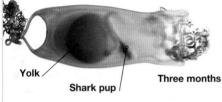

Yolk

Shark pup   **Three months**

1. Inside the egg of this small-spotted catshark, the embryo starts to form. It is attached to a yolk sac, from which it draws nourishment.

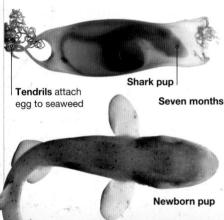

Tendrils attach egg to seaweed

Shark pup

Seven months

2. As the embryo grows and uses up the nourishment, the yolk sac shrinks. Water seeps into the egg, providing oxygen to the embryo.

Newborn pup

3. Eight to nine months after the egg is laid, the young catshark, called a pup, hatches and swims out into the sea.

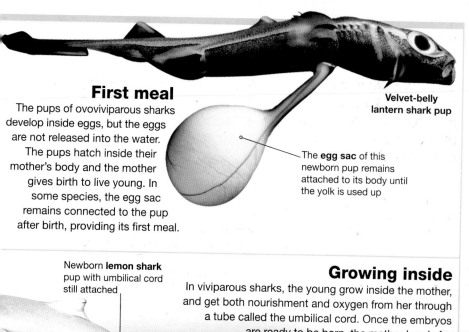

First meal

The pups of ovoviviparous sharks develop inside eggs, but the eggs are not released into the water. The pups hatch inside their mother's body and the mother gives birth to live young. In some species, the egg sac remains connected to the pup after birth, providing its first meal.

Velvet-belly lantern shark pup

The **egg sac** of this newborn pup remains attached to its body until the yolk is used up

Newborn **lemon shark** pup with umbilical cord still attached

Growing inside

In viviparous sharks, the young grow inside the mother, and get both nourishment and oxygen from her through a tube called the umbilical cord. Once the embryos are ready to be born, the mother heads for shallow waters to give birth.

Attack and defense

Speed, strength, and agility make sharks some of the deadliest predators on the planet. Different species of shark hunt in different ways. Some chase down their prey, while others hide and wait before ambushing their prey.

Pelagic thresher shark

The thresher's tail

Certain species of thresher shark use their long tails and speed to hunt prey. Swimming around a school of fish, the thresher herds them into a small area with its tail. Once the fish are packed together tightly, the shark swoops in and grabs one in its teeth.

Fast hunters

Big sharks such as makos and great whites rely on their speed to catch prey. They have been recorded chasing after seals and other prey at more than 25 mph (40 kph). They go so fast that they can leap out of the water completely.

Great white catching a seal

Mistaken identity

On rare occasions, sharks can attack humans. However, this is most likely to occur when they mistake us for their normal prey. For example, to a shark, a surfer looks a lot like a swimming seal.

Surfer on board

Seal

Ambush

Some sharks, such as angel sharks, which live near the seabed have evolved a particularly effective way to catch prey. They hide themselves in the sand and wait for fish to swim by. Once a fish is close enough, they strike fast.

Shark hunters

Sharks can also be prey themselves. Killer whales, or orcas, sometimes hunt sharks, including makos and great white sharks. The only defense these sharks have against the orcas is to use their speed and agility to escape.

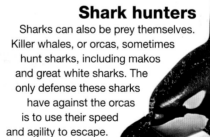

Orca

A shark's scales are like

teeth:

soft inside with a hard, enamel-like coating

DENTICLES
A shark's body is covered in small scales called denticles that act as protective armor against injuries. They also help to make the shark more streamlined so it can swim faster.

Habitats

Sharks live in every ocean in the world, and a few species even live in rivers. Some ocean-dwelling sharks move between warm and cool waters, but most are adapted to a particular kind of habitat, from shallow coastal waters to deep, open water.

Shark homes

Sharks live in different parts of the ocean at varying distances from land: coastal waters, continental shelves, slopes, and open water. Many coastal sharks inhabit coral reefs, where food is plentiful. The majority of sharks live in the shallow, food-rich waters above continental shelves or in the deeper waters above continental slopes, where the seabed drops away. Farther out to sea, sharks that live in open water are called pelagic. Many rely on speed to catch prey.

Coral reefs are home to sharks such as the whitetip reef shark.

Coastal waters are home to sharks such as salmon sharks and whitenose sharks.

Shortfin makos live in the open ocean, while great whites spend part of their time there.

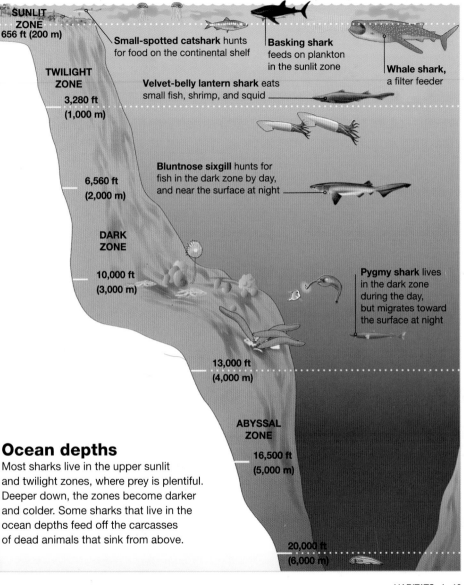

SUNLIT ZONE
656 ft (200 m)

Small-spotted catshark hunts for food on the continental shelf

Basking shark feeds on plankton in the sunlit zone

Whale shark, a filter feeder

TWILIGHT ZONE

3,280 ft (1,000 m)

Velvet-belly lantern shark eats small fish, shrimp, and squid

6,560 ft (2,000 m)

Bluntnose sixgill hunts for fish in the dark zone by day, and near the surface at night

DARK ZONE

10,000 ft (3,000 m)

Pygmy shark lives in the dark zone during the day, but migrates toward the surface at night

13,000 ft (4,000 m)

ABYSSAL ZONE

16,500 ft (5,000 m)

Ocean depths

Most sharks live in the upper sunlit and twilight zones, where prey is plentiful. Deeper down, the zones become darker and colder. Some sharks that live in the ocean depths feed off the carcasses of dead animals that sink from above.

20,000 ft (6,000 m)

Migration

Many sharks undertake long, regular journeys from one location to another, which is called migration. Different species of shark migrate for different reasons. Sometimes they move to find mates, sometimes to find a safe place to give birth. Some also migrate to the breeding grounds of their prey, where there is plenty of food available.

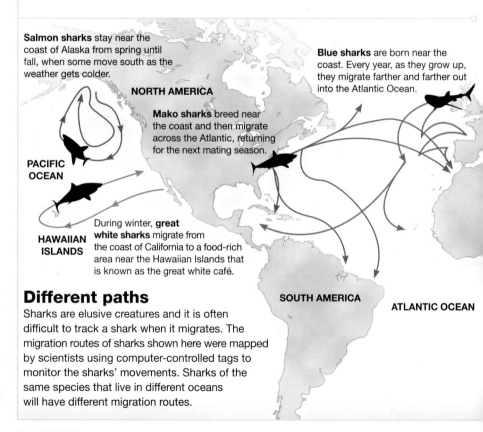

Salmon sharks stay near the coast of Alaska from spring until fall, when some move south as the weather gets colder.

NORTH AMERICA

Mako sharks breed near the coast and then migrate across the Atlantic, returning for the next mating season.

PACIFIC OCEAN

Blue sharks are born near the coast. Every year, as they grow up, they migrate farther and farther out into the Atlantic Ocean.

HAWAIIAN ISLANDS

During winter, **great white sharks** migrate from the coast of California to a food-rich area near the Hawaiian Islands that is known as the great white café.

SOUTH AMERICA

ATLANTIC OCEAN

Different paths

Sharks are elusive creatures and it is often difficult to track a shark when it migrates. The migration routes of sharks shown here were mapped by scientists using computer-controlled tags to monitor the sharks' movements. Sharks of the same species that live in different oceans will have different migration routes.

WHY SHARKS MIGRATE

To mate. Sharks migrate to breeding grounds to find mates.

To have pups. Female sharks often migrate to shallow waters to give birth.

For food. Sharks often follow the migration patterns of their prey.

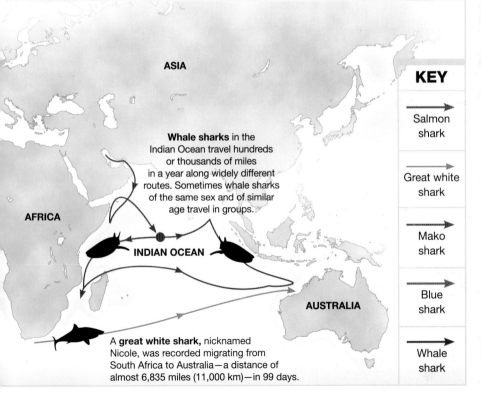

ASIA

AFRICA

Whale sharks in the Indian Ocean travel hundreds or thousands of miles in a year along widely different routes. Sometimes whale sharks of the same sex and of similar age travel in groups.

INDIAN OCEAN

AUSTRALIA

A **great white shark,** nicknamed Nicole, was recorded migrating from South Africa to Australia—a distance of almost 6,835 miles (11,000 km)—in 99 days.

KEY

→ Salmon shark

→ Great white shark

→ Mako shark

→ Blue shark

→ Whale shark

Sharks under threat

Sharks are hunted by people for their meat, fins, and sometimes just for sport. Many species of shark are endangered and some are at risk of becoming extinct. Efforts are now being made to protect the most endangered species.

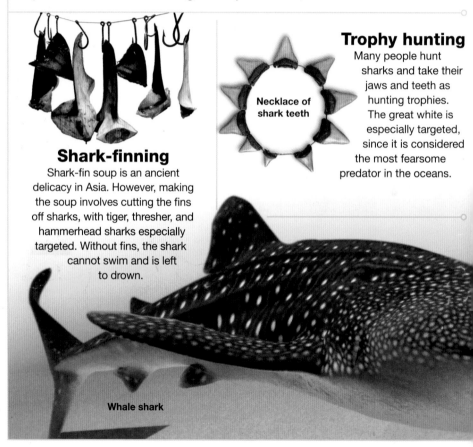

Shark-finning

Shark-fin soup is an ancient delicacy in Asia. However, making the soup involves cutting the fins off sharks, with tiger, thresher, and hammerhead sharks especially targeted. Without fins, the shark cannot swim and is left to drown.

Necklace of shark teeth

Trophy hunting

Many people hunt sharks and take their jaws and teeth as hunting trophies. The great white is especially targeted, since it is considered the most fearsome predator in the oceans.

Whale shark

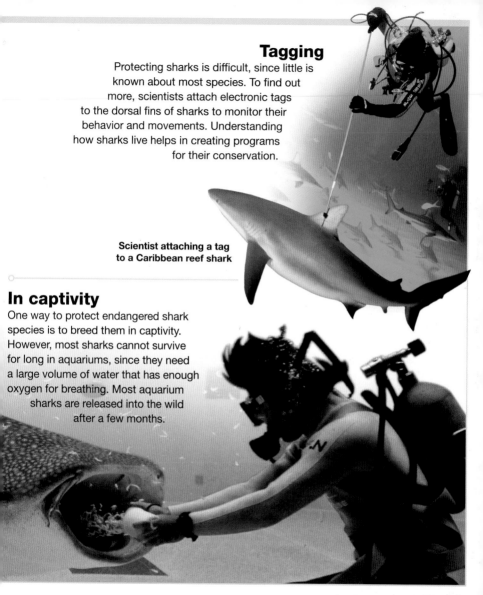

Tagging

Protecting sharks is difficult, since little is known about most species. To find out more, scientists attach electronic tags to the dorsal fins of sharks to monitor their behavior and movements. Understanding how sharks live helps in creating programs for their conservation.

Scientist attaching a tag to a Caribbean reef shark

In captivity

One way to protect endangered shark species is to breed them in captivity. However, most sharks cannot survive for long in aquariums, since they need a large volume of water that has enough oxygen for breathing. Most aquarium sharks are released into the wild after a few months.

Ancient sharks

Fossil evidence shows that sharks have existed for more than 400 million years. The most common type of shark fossils are teeth, because sharks shed many teeth in a lifetime. Some modern sharks are very similar to their ancestors because they have remained successful and have not changed their way of life.

Cladoselache

Although it lived more than 370 million years ago, the shape of this shark had features that resemble both modern frilled sharks and mackerel sharks. However, it did not have any scales on its body, except around the edges of its fins, mouth, and eyes.

SIZE   5 ft (1.5 m)

HABITAT   Open oceans

DISTRIBUTION   Fossils found in North America and Europe

Hybodus

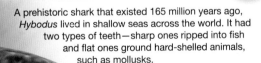

A prehistoric shark that existed 165 million years ago, *Hybodus* lived in shallow seas across the world. It had two types of teeth—sharp ones ripped into fish and flat ones ground hard-shelled animals, such as mollusks.

SIZE   8¼ ft (2.5 m)

HABITAT   Shallow seas

DISTRIBUTION   Fossils found in Asia, Europe, Africa, and North America

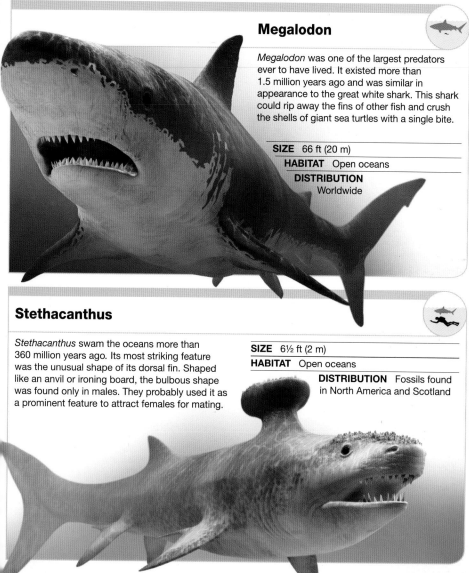

Megalodon

Megalodon was one of the largest predators ever to have lived. It existed more than 1.5 million years ago and was similar in appearance to the great white shark. This shark could rip away the fins of other fish and crush the shells of giant sea turtles with a single bite.

SIZE 66 ft (20 m)

HABITAT Open oceans

DISTRIBUTION
Worldwide

Stethacanthus

Stethacanthus swam the oceans more than 360 million years ago. Its most striking feature was the unusual shape of its dorsal fin. Shaped like an anvil or ironing board, the bulbous shape was found only in males. They probably used it as a prominent feature to attract females for mating.

SIZE 6½ ft (2 m)

HABITAT Open oceans

DISTRIBUTION Fossils found in North America and Scotland

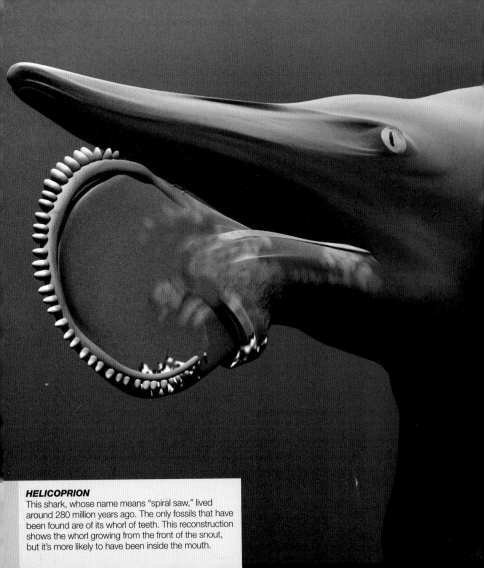

HELICOPRION
This shark, whose name means "spiral saw," lived around 280 million years ago. The only fossils that have been found are of its whorl of teeth. This reconstruction shows the whorl growing from the front of the snout, but it's more likely to have been inside the mouth.

Helicoprion had a whorl of 180 teeth like a **circular saw blade** the size of a dinner plate

Sharks

Sharks include the largest fish in the world—and some that are a tiny fraction of that size. There are more than 450 species that range from the dwarf lantern shark, which is a mere 8½ in (21 cm) long, to the whale shark, which can grow to 59 ft (18 m) long. Sharks are found in every ocean and some rivers. They are all carnivorous, but despite the fearsome reputation of some, including the great white shark (left), many are not dangerous to people.

CARIBBEAN REEF SHARK
Most sharks are active during the day, but the Caribbean reef shark often rests during the day and hunts at night.

Identifying sharks

There are more than 450 species of shark in the world today. The different species are placed in eight groups, or orders, based on particular body features, some of which are shown here.

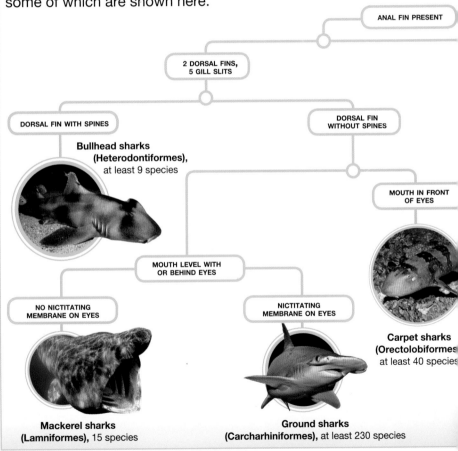

ANAL FIN PRESENT

2 DORSAL FINS, 5 GILL SLITS

DORSAL FIN WITH SPINES

DORSAL FIN WITHOUT SPINES

Bullhead sharks (Heterodontiformes), at least 9 species

MOUTH IN FRONT OF EYES

MOUTH LEVEL WITH OR BEHIND EYES

NO NICTITATING MEMBRANE ON EYES

NICTITATING MEMBRANE ON EYES

Carpet sharks (Orectolobiformes at least 40 species

Mackerel sharks (Lamniformes), 15 species

Ground sharks (Carcharhiniformes), at least 230 species

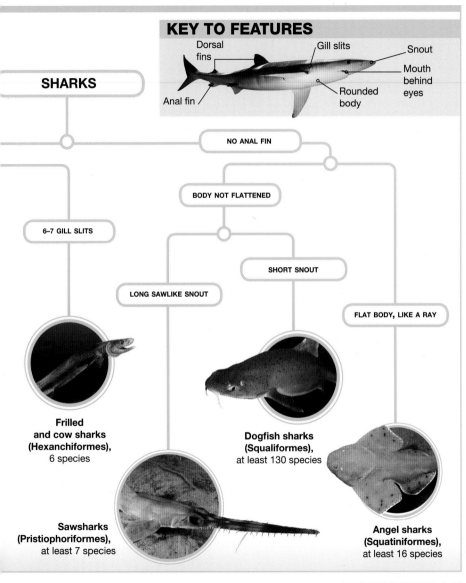

KEY TO FEATURES

Dorsal fins

Gill slits

Snout

Mouth behind eyes

Anal fin

Rounded body

SHARKS

NO ANAL FIN

BODY NOT FLATTENED

6–7 GILL SLITS

SHORT SNOUT

LONG SAWLIKE SNOUT

FLAT BODY, LIKE A RAY

Frilled and cow sharks (Hexanchiformes), 6 species

Dogfish sharks (Squaliformes), at least 130 species

Sawsharks (Pristiophoriformes), at least 7 species

Angel sharks (Squatiniformes), at least 16 species

FOCUS ON...
FEATURES
There are a number of features that set these sharks apart from others.

▲ Sharks of this order have six or seven gills, unlike other sharks, which have just five.

▲ Hexanchiformes have only one dorsal fin, but sharks in other orders have two.

▲ The frilled shark has a uniquely shaped tail, with ribbonlike frills.

Frilled and cow sharks

With features similar to the ancient sharks such as *Cladoselache*, the frilled sharks and cow sharks are put together in the order Hexanchiformes, which has just six species.

Frilled shark
Chlamydoselachus anguineus

Six gill slits on the neck

Named after the frilled edges to its gill slits, this weak-swimming shark is known to prey on injured or dying squid. However, it can also coil its body like a snake to launch a sudden strike, surprising its prey.

SIZE 3¼–3¾ ft (0.97–1.17 m)

HABITAT Continental shelves and slopes up to 3,280 ft (1,000 m) deep

DISTRIBUTION Western and eastern Atlantic Ocean and western, central, and eastern Pacific Ocean

Broadnose sevengill shark
Notorynchus cepedianus

The broadnose sevengill shark is easily identified, since it is one of the two shark species to have seven pairs of gills. It cruises near the seabed at a steady speed, before shooting forward to grab its prey.

SIZE 5–10 ft (1.5–3 m)

HABITAT Coastal waters and open oceans at least 446 ft (136 m) deep

DISTRIBUTION Southwestern and southeastern Atlantic Ocean, Indian Ocean, and western and eastern Pacific Ocean

Bluntnose sixgill shark
Hexanchus griseus

Also known as the cow shark, the bluntnose sixgill shark is extremely sensitive to light. During the day it swims around in the dark zone, migrating to the upper zones at night.

SIZE Up to 15¾ ft (4.8 m)

HABITAT Continental shelves and beyond, up to 6,560 ft (2,000 m) deep

DISTRIBUTION Western and eastern Atlantic Ocean, Indian Ocean, and Pacific Ocean

Sharpnose sevengill shark
Heptranchias perlo

This relatively small-sized species is more active at night. It feeds on small sharks, rays, and other small fish, and in turn is hunted by larger sharks.

SIZE 33½ in (85 cm)

HABITAT Continental shelves and slopes up to 3,280 ft (1,000 m) deep

DISTRIBUTION Atlantic Ocean, Indian Ocean, and Pacific Ocean

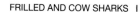

Dogfish sharks

The order of dogfish sharks, or Squaliformes, is made up of seven families. They are: dogfish sharks, bramble sharks, gulper sharks, sleeper sharks, lantern sharks, rough sharks, and kitefin sharks.

FOCUS ON...
FEATURES
Some dogfish sharks have unusual features.

Shortspine spurdog
Squalus mitsukurii

In some locations, this plain pearl-gray shark is known to migrate in large groups during winter months to breeding grounds for mating. It is also known as the green-eyed spurdog.

SIZE 2¼–3¼ ft (0.7–1 m)

HABITAT Continental shelves and beyond, up to 3,130 ft (954 m) deep

DISTRIBUTION Atlantic Ocean, Indian Ocean, and Pacific Ocean

Piked dogfish
Squalus acanthias

While most sharks live alone or in small groups, the piked dogfish gathers in groups of thousands. Once perhaps the most abundant shark in the world, its numbers have gradually decreased as it has been heavily overfished for its meat. The piked dogfish is now under threat in some locations.

SIZE 2–6½ ft (0.6–2 m)

HABITAT Continental shelves and beyond, up to 4,790 ft (1,460 m) deep

DISTRIBUTION Atlantic Ocean and Pacific Ocean

▲ The piked dogfish has a sharp spine on both dorsal fins that acts as a defense against predators. The spines are coated with a toxic slime, which may be venomous to some predators.

▲ Lantern sharks have special organs that produce light. This is called bioluminescence. It may be used by the fish to attract prey in the dark, deep waters in which it lives.

An adult piked dogfish can live for more than 100 years.

Dwarf gulper shark
Centrophorus atromarginatus

The dwarf gulper shark is often confused with its larger relative, the gulper shark, because both have a gray or gray-brown body color and widely spaced denticles. The dwarf gulper, however, can be recognized by the black markings on its fins, which the gulper shark lacks.

SIZE   23½ in (60 cm)

HABITAT   Continental shelves up to 1,480 ft (450 m) deep

DISTRIBUTION   Northern and eastern Indian Ocean and western Pacific Ocean

Smallfin gulper shark
Centrophorus moluccensis

The smallfin gulper shark preys on fish and crustaceans—hard-shelled animals including crabs, shrimp, and lobsters. It has been heavily overfished in some regions for its meat.

SIZE   3–4½ ft (0.9–1.4 m)

HABITAT   Continental shelves and slopes up to 2,690 ft (820 m) deep

DISTRIBUTION   Western and eastern Indian Ocean and western and southwestern Pacific Ocean

Mandarin dogfish
Cirrhigaleus barbifer

This dogfish seaches for prey by trailing its long barbels over the seabed. The barbels detect chemicals released by animals hidden under the sand, guiding the shark to its prey.

SIZE 2½–4 ft (0.8–1.2 m)

HABITAT Continental slopes up to 2,100 ft (640 m) deep

DISTRIBUTION Western Pacific Ocean

Longsnout dogfish
Deania quadrispinosum

The longsnout dogfish is dark brown, gray, or black. It has an extremely large snout and jaws armed with sharp cutting teeth.

SIZE 2½–3½ ft (0.8–1.1 m)

HABITAT Continental shelves and slopes up to 1,180 ft (360 m) deep

DISTRIBUTION Southeastern Atlantic Ocean, western and eastern Indian Ocean, and southwestern Pacific Ocean

Birdbeak dogfish
Deania calcea

The long, flattened snout of this shark has given it two interesting names—birdbeak dogfish and shovelnose spiny dogfish. An ovoviviparous species, it gives birth to up to 12 pups in one litter.

SIZE 2½–4 ft (0.8–1.2 m)

HABITAT Continental slopes up to 4,760 ft (1,450 m) deep

DISTRIBUTION Northern and eastern Atlantic Ocean, and northwestern, western, and eastern Pacific Ocean

Snout is almost as wide as body

Black dogfish
Centroscyllium fabricii

This shark has many jagged teeth with pointed ends that it uses to grab and crush the tough bodies of shellfish and small bony fish. Its dorsal fins are lined with grooved spines, which may contain mild toxins.

SIZE 1½–3¼ ft (0.5–1 m)

HABITAT Continental shelves and beyond, up to 5,250 ft (1,600 m) deep

DISTRIBUTION Western, eastern, and northern Atlantic Ocean

Black-belly lantern shark
Etmopterus lucifer

This small shark is often found in large schools deep in the ocean. Its belly is luminescent—it emits light. The glowing bellies of these lantern sharks may enable the fish to find one another in the dark waters, keeping the schools together.

SIZE Up to 16½ in (42 cm)

HABITAT Continental shelves and beyond, up to 4,460 ft (1,360 m) deep

DISTRIBUTION Western and southwestern Pacific Ocean

Smooth lantern shark
Etmopterus pusillus

The teeth in the upper jaw of the smooth lantern shark have up to three points, while those lining the lower jaw are single-pointed and knifelike. A bottom-dwelling shark, it feeds on fish eggs, squid, and deep-sea fish, such as lantern fish.

SIZE 20 in (50 cm)

HABITAT Continental slopes and beyond, up to 6,560 ft (2,000 m) deep

DISTRIBUTION
Western and eastern Atlantic Ocean, western Indian Ocean, and western Pacific Ocean

Velvet-belly lantern shark
Etmopterus spinax

The velvet-belly lantern shark is named after the color of its belly, which is much darker than the rest of its body. The young of this species live in shallow waters, but as they grow older, they move to deeper waters, where there is less competition for food.

SIZE Up to 16 in (40 cm)

HABITAT Continental shelves and beyond, up to 6,560 ft (2,000 m) deep

DISTRIBUTION Eastern Atlantic Ocean

Viper dogfish
Trigonognathus kabeyai

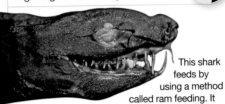

This shark feeds by using a method called ram feeding. It moves forward with its mouth open, captures the prey along with the water, and swallows it whole.

SIZE Up to 21¼ in (54 cm)

HABITAT Continental shelves and beyond, up to 1,180 ft (360 m) deep

DISTRIBUTION Central and northwestern Pacific Ocean

New Zealand lantern shark
Etmopterus baxteri

The diet of a New Zealand lantern shark consists of bony fish, squid, and crustaceans such as shrimp and crabs. However, since this shark grows in size it changes its diet, feeding more on bony fish than crustaceans.

Great lantern shark
Etmopterus princeps

This ovoviviparous shark does not have dots or dashes on its sides or the pale yellow spot on top of its head like many other lantern sharks. It is thought to be a bottom-dwelling feeder, based on its diet of squid, shrimp, and crabs.

SIZE 21½–29½ in (55–75 cm)

HABITAT Continental slopes up to 14,760 ft (4,500 m) deep

DISTRIBUTION Northern and southeastern Atlantic Ocean

SIZE 21½–34½ in (55–88 cm)

HABITAT Open waters and continental shelves and slopes up to 4,590 ft (1,400 m) deep

DISTRIBUTION Southwestern Pacific Ocean and southeastern Atlantic Ocean

Caudal fin lined with hooked denticles

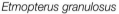

Slendertail lantern shark
Etmopterus molleri

This slender shark with a shiny belly is small enough to avoid capture—so small that it can slip through the holes in fishing nets and escape.

SIZE 18 in (46 cm)

HABITAT Continental shelves and slopes and open seas up to 2,820 ft (860 m) deep

DISTRIBUTION Western Indian Ocean and western and southwestern Pacific Ocean

Southern lantern shark
Etmopterus granulosus

The southern lantern shark has a broad head and lines of pointed denticles along its body. It has black markings on the underside of its body and tail. This shark feeds on bony fish, squid, shrimp, and crabs and is sometimes caught by shrimp fishers.

SIZE 16 in (41 cm)

HABITAT Continental shelves and beyond, up to 2,090 ft (637 m) deep

DISTRIBUTION Oceans around southern South America

Greenland shark
Somniosus microcephalus

Despite being poisonous, this shark's flesh is a delicacy in Iceland. The flesh is buried for about 12 weeks to extract the toxins.

Greenland sharks live in the freezing waters of the Arctic. They are slow swimmers and this helps them to save their energy in this environment. It is estimated that these sharks can live for up to 200 years.

SIZE 10–24 ft (3–7.3 m)

HABITAT Continental shelves and slopes up to 7,220 ft (2,200 m) deep

DISTRIBUTION Arctic Ocean and northern Atlantic Ocean

Portuguese dogfish
Centroscymnus coelolepis

The Portuguese dogfish is one of the deepest living sharks. Males usually live at great depths, while pregnant females confine themselves to shallower waters. Its sharp teeth allow the Portuguese dogfish to take bites out of large prey.

SIZE 2½–3¼ ft (0.75–1 m)

HABITAT Continental slopes and beyond, up to 12,140 ft (3,700 m) deep

DISTRIBUTION Atlantic Ocean, Indian Ocean, and western Pacific Ocean

Longnose velvet dogfish
Centroselachus crepidater

This shark is also called the golden dogfish. Its numbers are dwindling in some areas because of overfishing, since its liver oil is a source of squalene, a common ingredient in cosmetics and medicines.

SIZE 4¼ ft (1.3 m)

HABITAT Continental slopes up to 4,265 ft (1,300 m) deep

DISTRIBUTION Eastern Atlantic Ocean and parts of Indian Ocean and Pacific Ocean

Angular rough shark
Oxynotus centrina

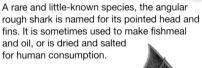

A rare and little-known species, the angular rough shark is named for its pointed head and fins. It is sometimes used to make fishmeal and oil, or is dried and salted for human consumption.

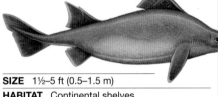

SIZE 1½–5 ft (0.5–1.5 m)

HABITAT Continental shelves and upper slopes up to 2,165 ft (660 m) deep

DISTRIBUTION Eastern Atlantic Ocean and the Mediterranean region, except the Black Sea

Sailfin rough shark
Oxynotus paradoxus

This deepwater shark migrates upward to the continental shelf during spring for reproduction. It eats fish and small bottom-dwelling shrimp and crabs.

SIZE Up to 4 ft (1.2 m)

HABITAT Continental slopes up to 2,360 ft (720 m) deep

DISTRIBUTION Northeastern Atlantic Ocean

Rough shark
Oxynotus bruniensis

Also known as the prickly dogfish, the skin of this shark is covered with large, prickly denticles. The rough shark has spearlike teeth in its upper jaw and bladelike teeth in its lower jaw that help it grasp and slice shrimp, crabs, and fish.

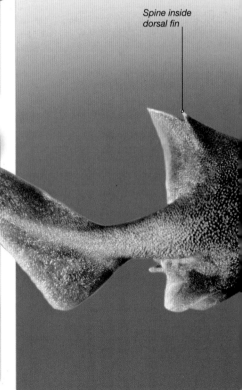

Spine inside dorsal fin

SIZE 23½–35 in (60–90 cm)

HABITAT Outer continental shelves
and beyond up to 3,510 ft (1,070 m) deep

DISTRIBUTION Southwestern Pacific Ocean

A weak swimmer, the rough shark relies on its large, oily liver to float above the seabed.

Kitefin shark
Dalatias licha

A solitary hunter, the kitefin shark preys on crabs, fish, rays, and other sharks. The large, knifelike teeth on its lower jaw form a continuous cutting edge, allowing it to take bites out of prey bigger than itself.

SIZE 2½–5¼ ft (0.8–1.6 m)

HABITAT Outer continental shelves and beyond, up to 5,905 ft (1,800 m) deep

DISTRIBUTION Eastern and western Atlantic Ocean, central and western Pacific Ocean, and western Indian Ocean

Cookiecutter shark
Isistius brasiliensis

The cookiecutter shark has a circular mouth with strong jaws and sawlike lower teeth, which can take circular cookie-shaped bites out of its prey. It has light-emitting organs on the underside of its body, which attract large predators to investigate. The cookiecutter then becomes the hunter, taking a bite out of the would-be predator.

SIZE Up to 22 in (56 cm)

HABITAT Around oceanic islands and open oceans up to 11,480 ft (3,500 m) deep

DISTRIBUTION Atlantic Ocean, Pacific Ocean, and Indian Ocean

Circular mouth with sharp teeth

Pygmy shark
Euprotomicrus bispinatus

The pygmy shark is one of the smallest sharks in the world. During the day, it swims in the dark zone to feed on squid, bony fish, and crustaceans, and swims to the water surface at night.

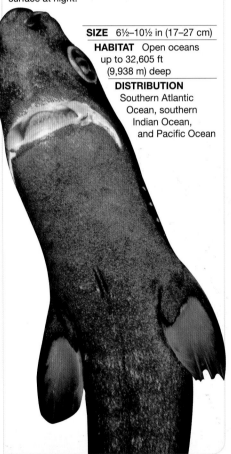

SIZE 6½–10½ in (17–27 cm)

HABITAT Open oceans up to 32,605 ft (9,938 m) deep

DISTRIBUTION Southern Atlantic Ocean, southern Indian Ocean, and Pacific Ocean

Sawsharks

The order of sawsharks, or Pristiophoriformes, contains at least seven species. The most distinctive feature of these sharks is the long, sawlike snout edged with teeth of varied length. They look similar to sawfish, a kind of ray, but sawfish teeth are more even.

Japanese sawshark
Pristiophorus japonicus

Like most sawsharks, this shark can search for prey by trailing its barbels across the seabed and using its snout to dig out hidden crabs and other crustaceans. It is found near the coasts of Japan, Korea, and China.

SIZE 2½–5 ft (0.8–1.5 m)

HABITAT Continental shelves and beyond, up to 2,625 ft (800 m) deep

DISTRIBUTION Northwestern Pacific Ocean

Tropical sawshark
Pristiophorus delicatus

This rare shark was only described as a separate species in 2008 and little is known about it. Tropical sawsharks live only in a small region off the coast of Queensland, Australia.

SIZE Up to 33½ in (85 cm)

HABITAT Outer continental shelves and upper slopes up to 1,330 ft (405 m) deep

DISTRIBUTION Northeastern Australia

FOCUS ON...
SNOUT
A sawshark's snout is a useful, if deadly, weapon.

▲ Sawsharks use the length of their snout to attack prey and defend against predators. The sharp teeth act as blades, cutting through flesh and inflicting a crippling wound.

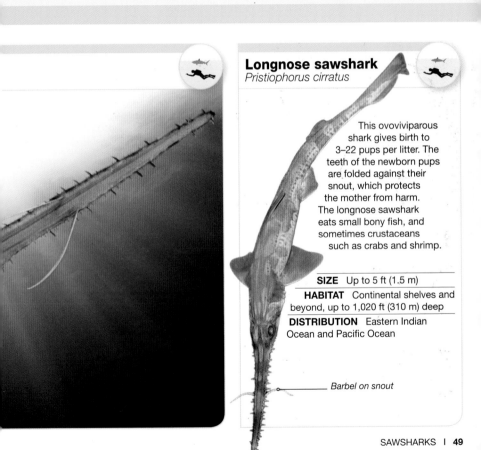

Longnose sawshark
Pristiophorus cirratus

This ovoviviparous shark gives birth to 3–22 pups per litter. The teeth of the newborn pups are folded against their snout, which protects the mother from harm. The longnose sawshark eats small bony fish, and sometimes crustaceans such as crabs and shrimp.

SIZE Up to 5 ft (1.5 m)

HABITAT Continental shelves and beyond, up to 1,020 ft (310 m) deep

DISTRIBUTION Eastern Indian Ocean and Pacific Ocean

Barbel on snout

FOCUS ON...
FEATURES
Angel sharks have
unusual adaptations
to help their hide-and-
strike hunting method.

▲ The flattened body and
camouflaged skin of an
angel shark allows it to hide,
unmoving, on the seabed.

▲ Angel sharks leave
their spiracles exposed
in order to breathe as
they lie under the sand.

▲ Unlike other sharks,
they can flatten their
dorsal fins and tail fins
onto the seabed.

Angel sharks

The 16 species that make up the order
Squatiniformes, or angel sharks, are very
different in appearance from other sharks.
They have flattened bodies and broad
pectoral fins, which allow them to hide
under sand in order to ambush prey.

Common angel shark ENDANGERED
Squatina squatina

The common angel shark is found on sandy or rocky
bottoms, or in seagrass beds, where it lies hidden
under the sand, waiting for prey. It feeds mainly on flatfish,
skates, crustaceans, and mollusks.

SIZE 2½–8 ft (0.8–2.4 m)

HABITAT Continental shelves up to
492 ft (150 m) deep

DISTRIBUTION Northern Atlantic Ocean,
Mediterranean Sea, and Black Sea

Japanese angel shark
Squatina japonica

The front half of this species looks like a ray, but the rear looks like a shark. Like other angel sharks, it can extend its "neck" to gulp down prey that swim overhead.

SIZE Up to 6½ ft (2 m)

HABITAT Continental shelves up to 984 ft (300 m) deep

DISTRIBUTION Northwestern Pacific Ocean

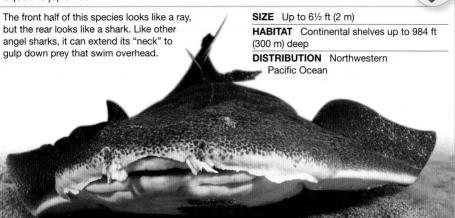

Australian angel shark
Squatina australis

The Australian angel shark is an ovoviviparous species that can give birth to up to 20 pups per litter. Its blunt snout and nostrils have fringed skin flaps that probably help detect prey by touch, taste, or smell.

SIZE Up to 5 ft (1.5 m)

HABITAT Continental shelves and beyond, up to 840 ft (256 m) deep

DISTRIBUTION Southeastern Indian Ocean and southwestern Pacific Ocean

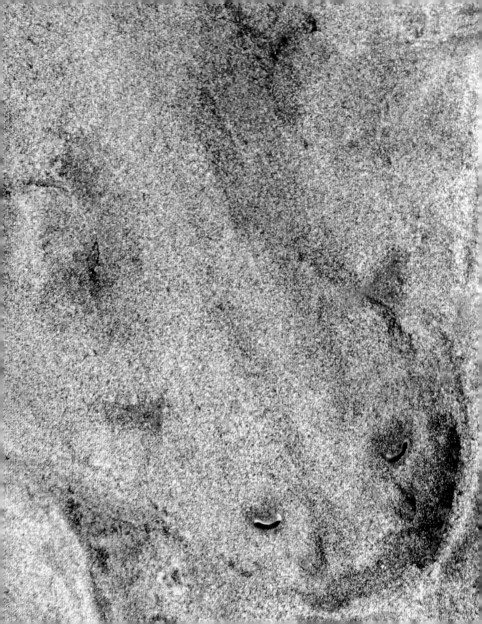

Hiding in the sand with barely its eyes exposed, the angel shark becomes
almost invisible

ANGEL SHARK

Angel sharks are benthic sharks, which means they live on the seabed. They are ambush predators, hiding in the sand to launch a surprise attack on prey. These sharks get their name because their pectoral and pelvic fins spread wide, like the wings of an angel.

Pacific angel shark
Squatina californica

It takes just one-tenth of a second for this shark to rise up from under the sand and snap up a passing fish in its jaws.

Commonly found in flat sands and reefs, this shark is recognized by the cone-shaped barbels on its snout. At night, the Pacific angel shark uses the light emitted by certain plankton to find its prey. When a fish passes through the swarm, the plankton give out light, which gives away its location to the hungry angel shark.

SIZE 3¼–5 ft (1–1.5 m)

HABITAT Continental shelves up to 656 ft (200 m) deep

DISTRIBUTION Northeastern and southeastern Pacific Ocean

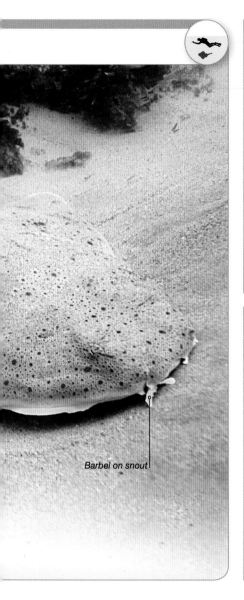

Barbel on snout

Sand devil
Squatina dumeril

Also known as the Atlantic angel shark, the sand devil is often mistaken for a ray because of its flat body and winglike fins. This fish is ovoviviparous, with up to 25 pups being born in each litter.

SIZE 3–5 ft (0.9–1.5 m)

HABITAT Continental shelves and beyond up to 820 ft (250 m) deep

DISTRIBUTION Northwestern Atlantic Ocean and Gulf of Mexico

Ornate angel shark
Squatina tergocellata

The ornate angel shark preys mainly on fish and squid, some of which have poisonous flesh. In order to keep the poison from affecting it, the angel shark swallows mud that acts as a buffer against the poison.

SIZE Up to 4½ ft (1.4 m)

HABITAT Continental shelves and beyond up to 1,310 ft (400 m) deep

DISTRIBUTION Southeastern Indian Ocean

Bullhead sharks

The nine species of bullhead shark form the order Heterodontiformes. These little blunt-headed sharks mostly feed on crustaceans, such as crabs and shrimp.

FOCUS ON...
FEATURES
Bullhead sharks have a combination of features that sets them apart.

Mexican hornshark
Heterodontus mexicanus

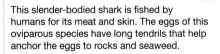

This slender-bodied shark is fished by humans for its meat and skin. The eggs of this oviparous species have long tendrils that help anchor the eggs to rocks and seaweed.

SIZE   16–20 in (40–50 cm)

HABITAT   Continental shelves up to 165 ft (50 m) deep

DISTRIBUTION   Eastern Pacific Ocean

Port Jackson shark
Heterodontus portusjacksoni

This shark has dark brown markings on a light gray-brown body. It is most active at night, when it feeds. It is not fished because its flesh and fins are considered to be of poor quality.

SIZE   29½ in (75 cm)

HABITAT   Coastal reefs up to 800 ft (245 m) deep

DISTRIBUTION   Eastern Indian Ocean and southwestern Pacific Ocean

▲ These sharks have a small spine on the front of each of their two dorsal fins.

▲ They have flat teeth at the back of their jaws for crushing the hard shells of their prey.

▲ The eggs of these sharks are spiral shaped, which allows them to become wedged in cracks, protecting them from predators.

Horn shark
Heterodontus francisci

The horn shark can survive more than 12 years in captivity—in aquariums to educate and entertain people, and where endangered sharks can be raised to preserve the species. This slow-moving predator prefers to hunt at night and take shelter during the day.

SIZE 22–24 in (56–61 cm)

HABITAT Continental shelves at least 500 ft (152 m) deep

DISTRIBUTION Eastern Pacific Ocean

The fin spines of the horn shark are used in making jewelry.

Zebra bullhead shark
Heterodontus zebra

This shark is named for its pattern of zebralike black stripes. It preys on other sharks' eggcases, biting through their hard covering with its teeth.

SIZE 2–4 ft (0.6–1.2 m)

HABITAT Continental shelves up to 720 ft (220 m) deep

DISTRIBUTION Western Pacific Ocean and eastern Indian Ocean

Japanese bullhead shark
Heterodontus japonicus

This popular Japanese aquarium pet can use its pectoral and pelvic fins to "walk" along the seabed while searching for food.

SIZE 2¼–4 ft (0.7–1.2 m)

HABITAT Continental shelves up to 120 ft (37 m) deep

DISTRIBUTION Northwestern Pacific Ocean

Galápagos bullhead shark
Heterodontus quoyi

A nocturnal predator, the Galápagos bullhead shark can often be seen resting on underwater ledges during the day. At night, it forages the seabed for prey, including shellfish, crabs, and mollusks.

SIZE 1½–3¼ ft (0.5–1 m)

HABITAT Coral reefs up to 100 ft (30 m) deep

DISTRIBUTION Eastern Pacific Ocean

Crested bullhead shark
Heterodontus galeatus

This rare bullhead shark can be recognized by the large ridges above its eyes and dark blotches on its body. The crested bullhead shark eats the eggcases of the Port Jackson shark.

SIZE 23½ in (60 cm)

HABITAT Continental shelves up to 305 ft (93 m) deep

DISTRIBUTION Western Pacific Ocean

The crested bullhead shark holds a tough eggcase with its front teeth and crushes it with those at the back to suck out the contents.

PATTERNS
This order gets
its name from
the skin patterns
in many of
the sharks.

▲ Zebra sharks have a
dotted, brown-on-white
pattern across their bodies.

▲ Each whale shark has
a unique pattern of spots
and stripes.

▲ A wobbegong's pattern
breaks up its outline,
helping it to hide in reefs.

Carpetsharks

The order of carpetsharks, or
Orectolobiformes, has more than
30 species. Sharks of this diverse
group range in size from the barbelthroat
(13 in/33 cm long) to the whale shark
(59 ft/18 m)—the world's largest fish.

Collared carpetshark
Parascyllium collare

This shark gets its name from the dark chocolate
brown or black collar that grows over its gills. The lack
of white spots on its collar makes it look different from
the necklace carpetshark.

SIZE   Up to 34¼ in (87 cm)

HABITAT   Continental shelves up to
525 ft (160 m) deep

DISTRIBUTION
Southwestern Pacific Ocean

Necklace carpetshark
Parascyllium variolatum

This small shark's bold, beautiful color pattern includes a speckled "necklace." It feeds mainly on bony fish, crabs, lobsters, crayfish, shrimp, krill, and mollusks.

SIZE Up to 35 in (90 cm)

HABITAT Continental shelves up to 590 ft (180 m) deep

DISTRIBUTION
Eastern Indian Ocean and southwestern Pacific Ocean

Bluegray carpetshark
Heteroscyllium colcloughi

Also known as Colclough's shark, the bluegray carpetshark is a rare species found only on the eastern coast of Australia. The young have black-and-white color patterns that fade with age.

SIZE 20–29½ in (50–75 cm)

HABITAT Continental shelves in inshore waters

DISTRIBUTION Western Pacific Ocean

Blind shark
Brachaelurus waddi

This small, stout shark gets its name from its habit of shutting its eyes when removed from water. The blind shark is known to have survived for up to 18 hours out of water.

SIZE 23½–28 in (60–70 cm)

HABITAT Coral reefs up to at least 360 ft (110 m) deep

DISTRIBUTION
Western Pacific Ocean

Whale shark
Rhincodon typus

Tawny nurse shark
Nebrius ferrugineus

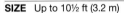

During the day, the tawny nurse shark can be found resting in gatherings of 20 or more sharks inside caves or on ledges. Hunting at night, the shark uses its strong jaws to suck out prey hiding inside holes and crevices.

SIZE Up to 10½ ft (3.2 m)

HABITAT Rocky or sandy seabeds up to 230 ft (70 m) deep

DISTRIBUTION Indo-Pacific (Red Sea and waters off East Africa to French Polynesian Islands)

Zebra shark
Stegostoma fasciatum

Zebra shark pups are patterned like zebras, with yellow stripes on a brown body. As they grow up, the pattern breaks up into brown spots on yellow.

The broad tail fin can be as long as rest of the body

The whale shark is the world's biggest fish. However, it is one of only three shark species to feed on tiny prey. It has a large mouth and eats plants and animals by filtering them through its comblike gill rakers.

SIZE 20–59 ft (6–18 m)

HABITAT Open oceans up to 2,300 ft (700 m) deep

DISTRIBUTION All tropical and warm temperate seas, except the Mediterranean Sea

Broad, flat head with a short snout

SIZE Up to 11½ ft (3.5 m)

HABITAT Coral reefs and rocky and sandy seabeds up to 210 ft (65 m) deep

DISTRIBUTION Indian Ocean and western Pacific Ocean

Nurse shark
Ginglymostoma cirratum

A nocturnal hunter, this shark spends the day resting in large groups on sand or in caves. After hunting, it returns to the same resting place every day. It has a small mouth but a large throat cavity to suck in its prey.

SIZE Up to 10 ft (3 m)

HABITAT Coastal reefs and sandy seabeds up to 430 ft (130 m) deep

DISTRIBUTION Western and eastern Atlantic Ocean and eastern Pacific Ocean

A whale shark's mouth
can grow to 5 ft (1.5 m)
wide and contain more
than **300 rows**
of tiny teeth, each no bigger
than a match head

WHALE SHARK
The gill rakers in the throat of a whale shark help it
to filter plankton, krill, small fish, and squid from
the water. However, it is not unusual for fish to
swim alongside the shark—its large size deters
other predators from pursuing them.

Japanese wobbegong
Orectolobus japonicus

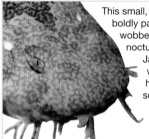

This small, boldly patterned wobbegong is nocturnal. The Japanese wobbegong hunts for shrimp, squid, octopuses and small fish. It eats shark eggcases, too.

SIZE   Up to 3¼ ft (1 m)

HABITAT   Coral reefs and rocky seabeds up to 656 ft (200 m) deep

DISTRIBUTION   Northwestern Pacific Ocean

Ornate wobbegong
Orectolobus ornatus

The ornate wobbegong shark uses its fanglike teeth to capture its prey, which include bony fish, sharks, and rays. The shark rests in groups by day and hunts at night.

SIZE
2–6 ft (0.6–1.8 m)

HABITAT   Coral reefs and rocky seabeds up to 328 ft (100 m) deep

DISTRIBUTION   Southeastern Indian Ocean and southwestern Pacific Ocean

Tasselled wobbegong
Eucrossorhinus dasypogon

This mainly nocturnal shark lives within a fixed range on the coral reefs. A solitary animal, the shark rests during the day inside caves and ledges, often eating the small fish that share its resting place.

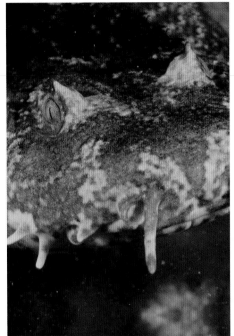

Cobbler wobbegong
Sutorectus tentaculatus

Irregular spots, colorful patterns, and wartlike growths give the cobbler wobbegong's body an irregular outline. This allows the shark to camouflage itself on the reefs, making it a very efficient ambush predator.

SIZE 28–35 in (70–90 cm)

HABITAT Coral reefs

DISTRIBUTION Southeastern Indian Ocean

SIZE Up to 4¼ ft (1.3 m)

HABITAT Coral reefs up to 130 ft (40 m) deep

DISTRIBUTION Eastern Indian Ocean and western Pacific Ocean

An ornate wobbegong can hold large prey in its mouth for days, impaled on its **fanglike teeth**

ORNATE WOBBEGONG SHARK
The ornate wobbegong is perfectly camouflaged among coral reefs and seaweed while it lies in wait to ambush its prey. It can use its fleshy barbels as lures to attract prey, which is quickly snapped up in its jaws.

Brownbanded bamboo shark
Chiloscyllium punctatum

The brownbanded bamboo shark is a popular aquarium shark as it needs little space to swim. In the wild it can survive for hours out of water when stranded by the outgoing tide.

SIZE Up to 4 ft (1.2 m)

HABITAT Coral reefs and nearby sandy seabeds

DISTRIBUTION Northeastern and eastern Indian Ocean and western Pacific Ocean

White-spotted bamboo shark
Chiloscyllium plagiosum

A common, yet little-known species, the white-spotted bamboo shark is mainly caught for its flesh and for use in Chinese medicines. It feeds on crustaceans and bony fish.

SIZE Up to 37½ in (95 cm)

HABITAT Coral reefs and nearby sandy seabeds

DISTRIBUTION Indian Ocean and western Pacific Ocean

Epaulette carpetshark
Hemiscyllium ocellatum

This shark uses its two front paddlelike fins to "walk" among the reefs, feeding on fish, worms, and crabs. On each side of its body, the shark has a large black spot ringed with white, which looks like an epaulette (soldiers' shoulder decoration).

SIZE   Up to 3½ ft (1.07 m)

HABITAT   Coral reefs up to 164 ft (50 m) deep

DISTRIBUTION   Eastern Indian Ocean and southwestern Pacific Ocean

Papuan epaulette carpetshark
Hemiscyllium hallstromi

The slender, eel-like body of the Papuan epaulette carpetshark allows it to move easily through confined spaces when searching for prey. It uses its muscular fins to wriggle or clamber over the seabed.

SIZE   Up to 29½ in (75 cm)

HABITAT   Coral reefs

DISTRIBUTION
Western central Pacific Ocean

The pectoral fins of this shark are so strong and muscular, it can easily raise itself up on them.

Milne Bay epaulette shark
Hemiscyllium michaeli

Until 2010, this epaulette shark was considered to be the same species as the Indonesian speckled carpetshark. This shark can be told apart from the Indonesian speckled carpetshark by the leopardlike brown spots on its back, as well as the well-defined black spot behind its head.

SIZE Up to 27 in (69.5 cm)

HABITAT Coral reefs and shallow sandy seabeds

DISTRIBUTION Western Pacific Ocean (Eastern Papua New Guinea)

Arabian carpetshark
Chiloscyllium arabicum

The Arabian carpetshark has a long, slender, and almost cylindrical body with a long tail. It moves over coral reefs in search of prey, using its barbels to sense chemicals in the water.

SIZE 20–28 in (50–70 cm)

HABITAT Coral reefs and sandy or rocky seabeds up to 328 ft (100 m) deep

DISTRIBUTION Northern Indian Ocean and Persian Gulf

Barbel is used for sensing prey

Hooded carpetshark
Hemiscyllium strahani

The head of this shark is paler than its body, giving it the appearance of wearing a hood. This species is under threat due to habitat destruction and capture for use as an aquarium fish.

SIZE 20–32 in (50–80 cm)

HABITAT Coral reefs up to 59 ft (18 m) deep

DISTRIBUTION Western Pacific Ocean (Eastern Papua New Guinea)

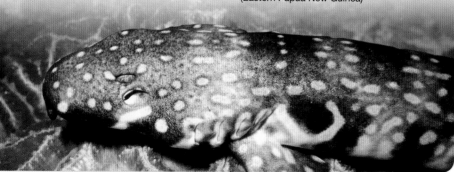

Mackerel sharks

The order of mackerel sharks, or Lamniformes, has existed for more than 120 million years. It includes some of the fastest sharks in the world, such as the great white and the shortfin mako.

FOCUS ON...
TEETH
The various species of this group have different type of teeth, depending on their prey.

Sandtiger shark
Carcharias taurus

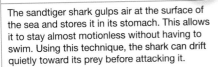

The sandtiger shark gulps air at the surface of the sea and stores it in its stomach. This allows it to stay almost motionless without having to swim. Using this technique, the shark can drift quietly toward its prey before attacking it.

SIZE 8¼–10½ ft (2.5–3.2 m)

HABITAT Continental shelves up to 626 ft (191 m) deep

DISTRIBUTION Warm oceans worldwide, except central and eastern Pacific Ocean

Goblin shark
Mitsukurina owstoni

The deep-living goblin shark can extend its jaws to reach out to prey. With a sucking motion, it draws the prey into its mouth and impales it on its teeth.

SIZE 8½–20¼ ft (2.6–6.2 m)

HABITAT Continental shelves and slopes at least 3,210 ft (979 m) deep

DISTRIBUTION Pacific Ocean, Atlantic Ocean, and Indian Ocean

▲ Basking sharks have tiny teeth, which they use to filter out small animals, such as plankton, from the water.

▲ The goblin shark has sharp teeth at the front of its mouth, which are used for stabbing squid, crabs, and fish.

▲ The teeth of the great white are triangular in shape, with serrated edges that help to tear off chunks of meat from its prey.

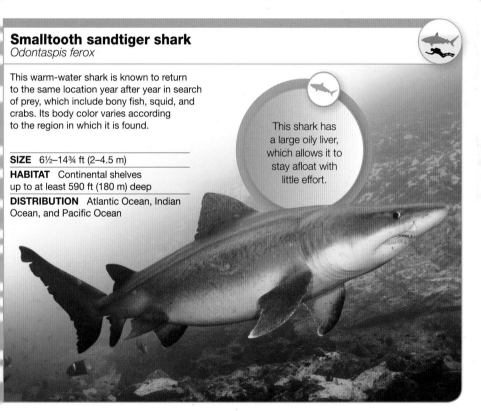

Smalltooth sandtiger shark
Odontaspis ferox

This warm-water shark is known to return to the same location year after year in search of prey, which include bony fish, squid, and crabs. Its body color varies according to the region in which it is found.

This shark has a large oily liver, which allows it to stay afloat with little effort.

SIZE 6½–14¾ ft (2–4.5 m)

HABITAT Continental shelves up to at least 590 ft (180 m) deep

DISTRIBUTION Atlantic Ocean, Indian Ocean, and Pacific Ocean

Crocodile shark
Pseudocarcharias kamoharai

This deepwater shark has large eyes for seeing in dim light. It extends its jaws to grab small fish and other prey with its stabbing teeth.

SIZE 2¼–3½ ft (0.7–1.1 m)

HABITAT Open oceans up to 1,935 ft (590 m) deep

DISTRIBUTION Tropical waters of the Atlantic Ocean, Indian Ocean, and Pacific Ocean

Megamouth shark
Megachasma pelagios

The megamouth shark hunts its prey in deep water during the day but moves upward at night, following its prey. This shark sucks in water through its mouth, filtering out animal plankton with its gill rakers.

SIZE 18–23¼ ft (5.5–7.1 m)

HABITAT Inshore, offshore, and oceanic waters up to 3,280 ft (1,000 m) deep

DISTRIBUTION Warm waters of the Atlantic Ocean, Indian Ocean, and Pacific Ocean

Basking shark
Cetorhinus maximus

Basking sharks are the second-largest fish in the ocean after whale sharks. They are filter feeders and in summer can be seen near the surface, swimming with their mouths wide open, taking in water laden with krill and other plankton.

A basking shark's liver makes up a quarter of its entire body weight.

SIZE 23–40½ ft (7–12.3 m)

HABITAT Inshore and offshore waters up to 4,150 ft (1,264 m) deep

DISTRIBUTION Temperate waters of the Atlantic Ocean, Pacific Ocean, and parts of the Indian Ocean

Female basking sharks may have pregnancies that last for
three years

BASKING SHARK
The basking shark gets its name from its habit of swimming slowly in sunlit waters near the ocean's surface. However, it can also dive to depths of 2,950 ft (900 m) to feed on plankton.

Thresher shark
Alopias vulpinus

This shark uses its long tail fin to round up shoals of fish and even stun them before killing them. Sometimes they attack in pairs. A very strong swimmer, the thresher shark is one of the few shark species known to jump fully out of water.

SIZE 9–20 ft (2.7–6 m)

HABITAT Continental shelves and beyond, up to at least 1,200 ft (365 m) deep

DISTRIBUTION Atlantic Ocean, Indian Ocean, and Pacific Ocean

Pelagic thresher shark
Alopias pelagicus

The pelagic thresher shark is the smallest of the thresher species. It is often confused with the thresher shark, since it is similar in appearance. The upper lobe of the tail fin is often as long as the shark's body. This ocean-living shark is known to swim to shallow waters in the morning where it allows certain species of fish to eat the dead skin and parasites on its body. This provides the shark with a cleaning service, while the fish get a meal.

SIZE 8¼–10 ft (2.5–3 m)

HABITAT Open oceans up to 500 ft (152 m) deep

DISTRIBUTION Indian Ocean and southern Pacific Ocean

Bigeye thresher shark
Alopias superciliosus

The large eyes of the bigeye thresher shark are adapted for hunting in low light. It hunts by looking for silhouettes of its prey in the dim light. This shark stays in deep water during the day and moves upward to feed in surface waters at night.

SIZE 10–15 ft (3–4.6 m)

HABITAT Continental shelves and beyond, up to at least 2,370 ft (723 m) deep

DISTRIBUTION Atlantic Ocean, Indian Ocean, and Pacific Ocean

A newborn pup of a pelagic thresher shark can be half as long as its mother.

Salmon shark
Lamna ditropis

As its name suggests, this shark feeds mainly on salmon. Like the great white, short fin mako, and porbeagle sharks, it can maintain a high body temperature, allowing it to hunt actively in cool water.

SIZE 6–10 ft (1.8–3 m)

HABITAT Cool coastal or oceanic waters up to 820 ft (250 m) deep

DISTRIBUTION Northern Pacific Ocean

Porbeagle shark
Lamna nasus

Porbeagle sharks can migrate long distances of 1,240 miles (2,000 km) or more, traveling between feeding areas and breeding areas.

SIZE 5–10 ft (1.5–3 m)

HABITAT Inshore to offshore waters up to 1,215 ft (370 m) deep

DISTRIBUTION Southern Atlantic Ocean, southern Indian Ocean, southern Pacific Ocean, and Southern Ocean

Great white shark
Carcharodon carcharias

One of the world's largest predators, the great white shark is not always easily noticed by its prey because of its colouring. When prey looks up from below, the shark's white belly looks like a patch of sunlight. When seen from the side, the light reflects differently off the belly compared to the grey back, breaking up the shark's outline. This is known as countershading.

SIZE 11½–21 ft (3.5–6.4 m)

HABITAT Coastal, inshore, and offshore waters up to 4,000 ft (1,220 m) deep

DISTRIBUTION Cool to warm waters of the Atlantic Ocean, Indian Ocean, and Pacific Ocean

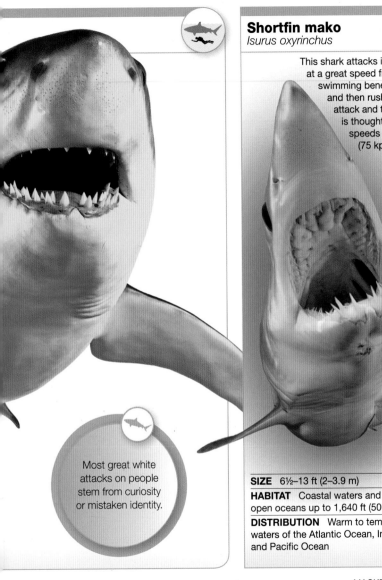

Shortfin mako
Isurus oxyrinchus

This shark attacks its prey at a great speed from below, swimming beneath its prey and then rushing upward to attack and tear off flesh. It is thought to reach speeds of 46.5 mph (75 kph).

Most great white attacks on people stem from curiosity or mistaken identity.

SIZE 6½–13 ft (2–3.9 m)

HABITAT Coastal waters and open oceans up to 1,640 ft (500 m) deep

DISTRIBUTION Warm to temperate waters of the Atlantic Ocean, Indian Ocean, and Pacific Ocean

GREAT WHITE SHARK
The great white shark is one of the most efficient predators in the world. Like many other sharks, its ampullae of Lorenzini can detect the weak electrical signals of its prey when close. It can probably sense electric fields that are a million times weaker than humans can sense.

A great white shark can sniff out a single drop of **blood** in 26.4 gallons (100 liters) of water

Ground sharks

With more than 230 species, ground sharks, or Cacharhiniformes, form the largest order. It is made up of eight families, including catsharks and hammerheads.

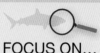

Longnose catshark
Apristurus kampae

Newborn pups have two rows of enlarged denticles on their backs that help them break out of the egg case. These disappear soon after birth.

This is an oviparous species that feeds on shrimp, squid, and small fish. Since it lives in deep waters, the longnose catshark is rarely caught and so very little is known about it.

SIZE Up to 20½ in (52 cm)

HABITAT Continental slopes up to 6,235 ft (1,900 m) deep

DISTRIBUTION Northeastern and southeastern Pacific Ocean

▲ The roughskin catshark is found in deep waters beyond the continental shelves.

▲ The coral catshark prefers to spend its time in holes and caves in coral reefs.

▲ The gray reef shark can be found hunting for prey over reefs and near coasts.

Deepwater catshark
Apristurus profundorum

The deepwater catshark is a small, sluggish fish with a thick, flattened snout. Its skin has a feltlike texture, which gives it a fuzzy appearance. It has rather prominent gill slits and a long tail fin. It feeds on crustaceans, squid, and small fish.

SIZE At least 20½ in (50 cm)

HABITAT Continental slopes up to 5,740 ft (1,750 m) deep

DISTRIBUTION Western and eastern Atlantic Ocean

Roughskin catshark
Apristurus ampliceps

The roughskin catshark has a brown or black-brown body. Like other deepwater sharks, it is rarely caught, since it lives in a deep zone where fishing nets almost never reach.

SIZE 26¼–34 in (67–86 cm)

HABITAT Continental slopes up to 4,920 ft (1,500 m) deep

DISTRIBUTION Southwestern Pacific Ocean

Gray spotted catshark
Asymbolus analis

This little-researched catshark is found near southeastern Australia. It is caught as bycatch by trawler fishermen and may be vulnerable to unintended overfishing.

SIZE 18–23½ in (45–60 cm)

HABITAT Continental shelves up to 575 ft (175 m) deep

DISTRIBUTION Western Pacific Ocean

Western spotted catshark
Asymbolus occiduus

This catshark is found only around southwestern Australia. Like other small catsharks, it can only be trapped by nets with small meshes. Being quite numerous, it is less vulnerable than the gray spotted catshark to accidental overfishing.

Orange spotted catshark
Asymbolus rubiginosus

Often caught as bycatch, this oviparous catshark's numbers are less affected by trawling because of its continuous egg-laying cycle. The next batch of eggs are laid before, as soon as, or just after the previous pups hatch. This helps maintain its numbers.

SIZE 14–21½ in (35–55 cm)

HABITAT Continental shelves and beyond up to 1,770 ft (540 m) deep

DISTRIBUTION Western Pacific Ocean

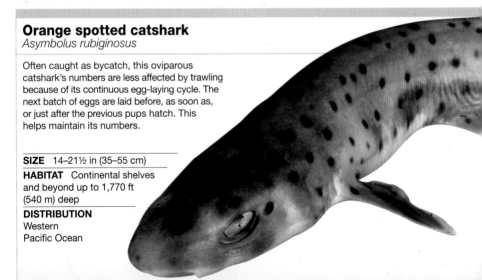

SIZE 23–23½ in (58–60 cm)

HABITAT Outer continental shelves up to 322–820 ft (98–250 m) deep

DISTRIBUTION Eastern Indian Ocean

Coral catshark
Atelomycterus marmoratus

The coral catshark hides in reefs and remains inactive during the day, coming out at dusk and at night to hunt for squid and small bony fish. This small shark is harmless and attractive, and so is a popular choice for aquariums.

SIZE 16–28 in (40–70 cm)

HABITAT Coral reefs

DISTRIBUTION Western Pacific Ocean

The number of females carrying eggs is highest in spring, intermediate in the fall, and lowest in winter.

Blackmouth catshark
Galeus melastomus

The blackmouth catshark spends its time near the muddy seabed. It relies heavily on its ampullae of Lorenzini to hunt prey in these dark waters. Young sharks tend to swim in shallower waters than the adults.

SIZE   14–32 in (35–80 cm)

HABITAT   Continental shelves and beyond up to 3,280 ft (1,000 m) deep

DISTRIBUTION   Northeastern Atlantic Ocean and Mediterranean Sea

Swell shark
Cephaloscyllium ventriosum

Like the draughtsboard catshark, this shark swallows water to prevent predators from pulling it out of its hiding place. During an attack, it may also hold its tail in its mouth to stop other fish from getting hold of it.

SIZE 2½–3¼ ft (0.8–1 m)

HABITAT Continental shelves up to 1,510 ft (460 m) deep

DISTRIBUTION Eastern Pacific Ocean

When under threat, the swell shark can suck in enough water to double its size.

Draughtsboard catshark
Cephaloscyllium isabellum

The draughtsboard catshark defends itself against predators by hiding inside holes among rocks or reefs and sucking in water. This inflates its body and wedges it inside the hole, making it difficult for a predator to pull it out.

SIZE 2–5 ft (0.6–1.5 m)

HABITAT Sandy and rocky seabeds up to 2,210 ft (673 m) deep

DISTRIBUTION Coastal and offshore waters around New Zealand

Striped catshark
Poroderma africanum

This shark is also known as the pajama shark because of the dark stripes on its body that run from nose to tail. These stripes help it to blend in with the surrounding rocks and reefs.

SIZE   23½–37½ in (60–95 cm)

HABITAT   Coastal and offshore areas up to 920 ft (280 m) deep

DISTRIBUTION   Southeastern Atlantic Ocean and southwestern Indian Ocean

Leopard catshark
Poroderma pantherinum

Dark shyshark
Haploblepharus pictus

The dark shyshark gets its name from its habit of curling into a ring with its tail covering its eyes when threatened. Until recently, the dark shyshark was regarded by some to be the same species as the puffadder shyshark.

The markings on this shark depend on its age and location. Newborn pups have black spots, but as they grow, these spots can become smaller, and sometimes merge into lines. Densely spotted sharks are found off the Eastern Cape of South Africa.

SIZE Up to 33 in (84 cm)

HABITAT Rocky seabeds up to 820 ft (250 m) deep

DISTRIBUTION Southwestern Indian Ocean and southeastern Atlantic Ocean

SIZE Up to 23½ in (60 cm)

HABITAT Rocky seabeds up to 115 ft (35 m) deep

DISTRIBUTION Southeastern Atlantic Ocean and western Indian Ocean around South Africa

Puffadder shyshark
Haploblepharus edwardsii

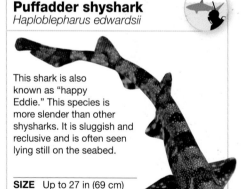

This shark is also known as "happy Eddie." This species is more slender than other shysharks. It is sluggish and reclusive and is often seen lying still on the seabed.

SIZE Up to 27 in (69 cm)

HABITAT Sandy or rocky seabeds up to 427 ft (130 m) deep

DISTRIBUTION Southeastern Atlantic Ocean and southwestern Indian Ocean

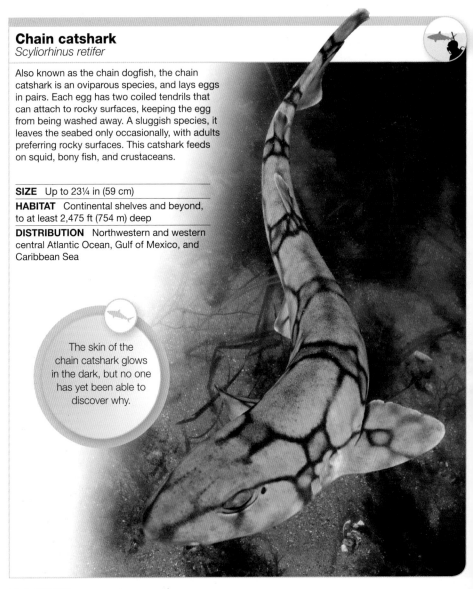

Chain catshark
Scyliorhinus retifer

Also known as the chain dogfish, the chain catshark is an oviparous species, and lays eggs in pairs. Each egg has two coiled tendrils that can attach to rocky surfaces, keeping the egg from being washed away. A sluggish species, it leaves the seabed only occasionally, with adults preferring rocky surfaces. This catshark feeds on squid, bony fish, and crustaceans.

SIZE Up to 23¼ in (59 cm)

HABITAT Continental shelves and beyond, to at least 2,475 ft (754 m) deep

DISTRIBUTION Northwestern and western central Atlantic Ocean, Gulf of Mexico, and Caribbean Sea

The skin of the chain catshark glows in the dark, but no one has yet been able to discover why.

Small-spotted catshark
Scyliorhinus canicula

This shark's skin has a sandpaperlike texture

The small-spotted catshark, also known as the lesser spotted dogfish, is known to use its denticles when feeding. After grasping prey in its jaws, the shark curls its tail toward its mouth, hooking its denticles into the prey. It then flicks its head back, shredding pieces of flesh from the prey.

SIZE 23½–28 in (60–70 cm)

HABITAT Continental shelves up to at least 330 ft (100 m) deep

DISTRIBUTION Northeastern and eastern Atlantic Ocean

Cloudy catshark
Scyliorhinus torazame

One of the few shark species to be successfully bred in captivity, the cloudy catshark is often found in aquariums. It is a bottom-dweller, found among rocky reefs. It migrates only short distances.

SIZE 19 in (48 cm)

HABITAT Continental shelves up to at least 1,050 ft (320 m) deep

DISTRIBUTION Northwestern and western central Pacific Ocean

SMALL-SPOTTED CATSHARK EGGS
The small-spotted catshark is an oviparous species that lays eggs in shallow waters near coasts and reefs. Also known as mermaid's purses, the eggs have tendrils that wrap around rocks and seaweed, anchoring the eggs in place.

A mermaid's purse

shark egg can remain attached
to a rock for up to 11 months
while the embryo grows inside

Soupfin shark
Galeorhinus galeus

Also known as the tope, school, or snapper shark, this fish is found in cool to subtropical seas around much of the world. The soupfin shark is slow to mature and is at risk of being overfished.

SIZE 4–6¼ ft (1.2–1.9 m)

HABITAT Continental shelves and slopes up to 1,640 ft (500 m) deep

DISTRIBUTION Southwestern and eastern Atlantic Ocean, western and eastern Indian Ocean, and western and eastern Pacific Ocean

Brown smoothhound
Mustelus henlei

This small, slender shark is a fast-growing species. It swims actively when kept in an aquarium and is one of the most successful sharks to be bred in captivity. It gives birth to 3–5 pups in a litter.

SIZE 1½–3¼ ft (0.5–1 m)

HABITAT Continental shelves up to 656 ft (200 m) deep

DISTRIBUTION Eastern Pacific Ocean

Starry smoothhound
Mustelus asterias

An ovoviviparous species, the starry smoothhound gives birth to a litter of 7–15 pups after a 12-month gestation period. Although it spends most of its time away from the coast, many starry smoothhounds migrate to pupping grounds near the shore during summer.

SIZE 2½–5 ft (0.8–1.5 m)

HABITAT Continental shelves up to 656 ft (200 m) deep

DISTRIBUTION Northeastern Atlantic Ocean

Leopard shark
Triakis semifasciata

Saddle-shaped pattern on the back

The leopard shark lives in oxygen-poor waters, where there is less competition for food, and preys on shrimp and fish eggs. It absorbs oxygen more efficiently than other sharks because its red blood cells, which carry oxygen in the bloodstream, are smaller and more numerous.

SIZE 3¼–7 ft (1–2.1 m)

HABITAT Continental shelves up to 164 ft (50 m) deep

DISTRIBUTION Northeastern, eastern, and central Pacific Ocean

Spotted estuary smoothhound
Mustelus lenticulatus

This shark is a highly migratory species. Males, females, and sharks of the same size form separate schools (groups). Also known as the rig shark or lemonfish, its meat is served in fish and chip restaurants in New Zealand.

SIZE 2¾–5 ft (0.85–1.5 m)

HABITAT Continental shelves and beyond, up to 2,820 ft (860 m) deep

DISTRIBUTION Waters around New Zealand

Whiskery shark
Furgaleus macki

During the 1970s, the whiskery shark was heavily fished in Australia for its meat, leading to a 70 percent decrease in population. Strict conservation measures by the Australian government have allowed the population to return.

SIZE 3½–5 ft (1.1–1.5 m)

HABITAT Continental shelves up to 720 ft (220 m) deep

DISTRIBUTION Eastern Indian Ocean, near southern Australia

Snaggletooth shark
Hemipristis elongatus

Despite its hooked and dangerous-looking teeth, the snaggletooth is harmless to humans.

This shark gets its name from its jagged, sawlike teeth. The lower teeth protrude outward even when its mouth is closed. Its meat and liver, which are a rich source of vitamins, are sold for human consumption.

SIZE 3½–8 ft (1.1–2.4 m)

HABITAT Continental shelves up to 427 ft (130 m) deep

DISTRIBUTION Indian Ocean and western Pacific Ocean

Hooktooth shark
Chaenogaleus macrostoma

This shark is fished for food by humans and its by-products are processed into fishmeal. It feeds on small fish and crustaceans. This viviparous species gives birth to four pups per litter.

SIZE 2½–4 ft (0.8–1.25 m)

HABITAT Continental shelves up to at least 194 ft (59 m) deep

DISTRIBUTION Indian Ocean and northwestern and western central Pacific Ocean

Sicklefin weasel shark
Hemigaleus microstoma

Found in shallow waters, this shark feeds mainly on octopuses and crustaceans. The sicklefin weasel shark may be under threat from overfishing in some localities.

SIZE 2–3½ ft (0.6–1.1 m)

HABITAT Continental shelves up to 558 ft (170 m) deep

DISTRIBUTION Indian Ocean and northwestern and western central Pacific Ocean

Spinner shark
Carcharhinus brevipinna

The spinner shark gets its name from its actions when hunting. It sometimes charges through a school of fish from below, spinning through the air as it does so.

SIZE 5¼–9 ft (1.6–2.8 m)

HABITAT Coastal waters and offshore up to 328 ft (100 m) deep

DISTRIBUTION Western and eastern Atlantic Ocean, western Pacific Ocean, and western and eastern Indian Ocean

Galápagos shark
Carcharhinus galapagensis

The Galápagos shark lives and hunts around oceanic islands, sometimes swimming long distances from one island to another in search of prey. It can often be seen in schools around seamounts (mountains submerged in water).

SIZE 5½–12 ft (1.7–3.7 m)

HABITAT Around oceanic islands in waters up to 590 ft (180 m) deep

DISTRIBUTION Western and eastern Atlantic Ocean, western Indian Ocean, and western, central, and eastern Pacific Ocean

Silky shark
Carcharhinus falciformis

Newborn silky sharks spend their early months in sheltered reefs. As they grow older, they begin venturing out into open waters, moving in groups for protection. A keen sense of hearing helps them detect even the slightest noise made by their prey.

SIZE 6½–10 ft (2–3 m)

HABITAT Open oceans up to 1,640 ft (500 m) deep

DISTRIBUTION Atlantic Ocean, Indian Ocean, and Pacific Ocean

Silvertip shark
Carcharhinus albimarginatus

The silvertip shark has an unusual method of defense when threatened by a rival or predator. The shark first swims away to a distance of 49 ft (15 m) and then moves rapidly toward the threat. Once it is about 11½ ft (3.5 m) away, it stops, turns to its side, and shivers, displaying the white markings on its fins as a warning to back off. If the rival or predator does not move away, the shark closes in and may slash it with its teeth.

SIZE 6½–8¼ ft (2–2.5 m)

HABITAT Continental shelves and beyond, up to 2,625 ft (800 m) deep

DISTRIBUTION Western Indian Ocean and western, central, and eastern Pacific Ocean

Narrowly rounded or pointed fin with a white tip

BRONZE WHALER SHARK
From May to July, billions of sardines migrate in masses up to 4¼ miles (7 km) long, which act as the perfect pantry for the bronze whaler. Bony fish such as sardines make up the main part of this predator's diet, along with squid and small sharks.

Schools of bronze whaler sharks follow the

sardine run,

the annual migration of billions of sardines along the east coast of South Africa

Blue shark
Prionace glauca

The blue shark is most active during the evening and at night. It is probably the most heavily fished shark in the world and is caught mainly for its fins. It is highly migratory, traveling long distances in search of food and to mate.

SIZE
Up to 11–13 ft
(3.3–4 m)

HABITAT Continental shelves
and beyond, up to 1,150 ft (350 m) deep

DISTRIBUTION Atlantic Ocean, Indian Ocean,
and Pacific Ocean

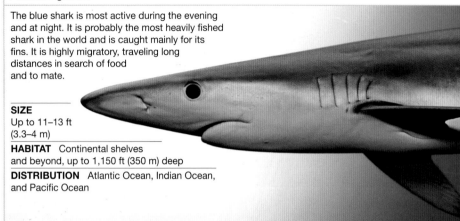

Oceanic whitetip shark
Cacharhinus longimanus

Although it usually hunts alone, the oceanic whitetip shark can form groups where plenty of food is available. When competing with other species of shark for food, it becomes aggressive toward them. It is known to follow ships and can be dangerous to humans.

SIZE Up to 12¼ ft (3.75 m)

HABITAT Open oceans up to 656 ft
(200 m) deep

DISTRIBUTION Atlantic Ocean,
Indian Ocean, and Pacific Ocean

Dusky shark
Carcharhinus obscurus

The dusky shark matures slowly, with females only breeding when they are at least 15 years old. They then mate every other year. Slow breeding puts them at risk of overfishing.

SIZE 11¼–13 ft (3.4–4 m)

HABITAT Continental shelves and beyond, up to 1,310 ft (400 m) deep

DISTRIBUTION Western and eastern Atlantic Ocean, Indian Ocean, and western and eastern Pacific Ocean

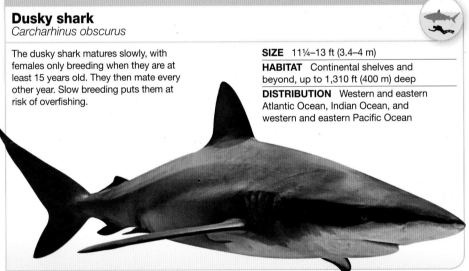

Sandbar shark
Carcharhinus plumbeus

The sandbar shark is one of the world's largest coastal sharks. It is hunted for its meat, leather, and oil.

SIZE 6½–8¼ ft (2–2.5 m)

HABITAT Continental shelves and beyond, up to 920 ft (280 m) deep

DISTRIBUTION Warm waters of the Atlantic Ocean, Indian Ocean, and Pacific Ocean

Blacknose shark
Carcharhinus acronotus

This small, schooling shark gets its name from the black blotch found on the tip of its snout. A fast, agile swimmer, the blacknose shark's speed sometimes allows it to snatch food from bigger sharks.

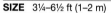

SIZE 3¼–6½ ft (1–2 m)

HABITAT Continental shelves up to 210 ft (64 m) deep

DISTRIBUTION Western Atlantic Ocean

Sharptooth lemon shark
Negaprion acutidens

Though similar in appearance to the lemon shark, the sharptooth lemon shark can be recognized by its sickle-shaped pectoral fins. This shark is thought to be nonmigratory, since it appears to remain in small areas throughout the year.

SIZE 7¼–10 ft (2.2–3 m)

HABITAT Rocky, sandy, or muddy seabeds up to 98 ft (30 m) deep

DISTRIBUTION Indian Ocean and western and central Pacific Ocean

Tiger shark
Galeocerdo cuvier

A young tiger shark has dark stripes on its body similar to those on a tiger. These fade as the shark matures. Small remora fish often follow or attach themselves to tiger sharks, feeding on dead skin and parasites on the sharks' bodies.

SIZE 13–21½ ft (4–6.5 m)

HABITAT Coastal and offshore waters up to 459 ft (140 m) deep

DISTRIBUTION Warm waters of the Atlantic Ocean, Indian Ocean, and Pacific Ocean

Lemon shark
Negaprion brevirostris

This is a stocky, powerful shark, named for its pale yellow-brown to gray skin. It does not have any markings on its body, which allows it to blend in perfectly with its coastal habitat.

SIZE 6½–10 ft (2–3 m)

HABITAT Coastal waters up to 295 ft (90 m) deep

DISTRIBUTION Western and eastern Atlantic Ocean

Young lemon sharks can lose a
whole set of teeth,
one by one, every 10 days.
A tooth from the row behind
moves forward to fill the gap

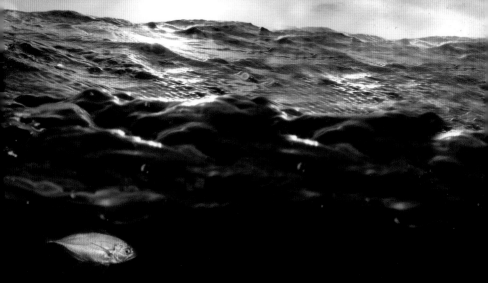

LEMON SHARK
Female lemon sharks give birth to up to 17 pups and leave them to fend for themselves as soon as they are born. The young sharks stay in shallow nursery waters for several years until they are large enough to swim farther offshore to find their own mates.

Gray reef shark
Carcharhinus amblyrhynchos

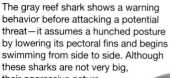

The gray reef shark shows a warning behavior before attacking a potential threat—it assumes a hunched posture by lowering its pectoral fins and begins swimming from side to side. Although these sharks are not very big, their aggressive nature enables them to ward off most larger sharks.

SIZE 4–6¼ ft (1.2–1.9 m)

HABITAT Inshore, offshore, and oceanic waters up to 459 ft (140 m) deep

DISTRIBUTION Indian Ocean and western and central Pacific Ocean

Caribbean reef shark
Carcharhinus perezi

During the day, this shark will sometimes rest for short periods under ledges or in caves. When swimming near coral reefs, they are a popular spectacle for divers.

SIZE 6½–9¾ ft (2–2.95 m)

HABITAT Continental shelves up to 98 ft (30 m) deep

DISTRIBUTION Western Atlantic Ocean

Blacktip reef shark
Carcharhinus melanopterus

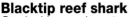

The prominent black-tipped fins and light brown to gray upper body of the blacktip reef shark make it easily recognizable. This timid shark rarely poses a danger to humans.

SIZE Up to 5¼ ft (1.6 m)

HABITAT Coral reefs up to 33 ft (10 m) deep

DISTRIBUTION Indian Ocean, central and western Pacific Ocean, and part of the Mediterranean Sea

Bull shark
Carcharhinus leucas

The bull shark is found across the world, not only in oceans but in rivers as well. It is usually a solitary creature and aggressively attacks any animal that enters its territory.

SIZE 10–11¼ ft (3–3.4 m)

HABITAT Coastal waters up to 500 ft (152 m) deep and in freshwater rivers and lakes

DISTRIBUTION Warm waters of the Atlantic Ocean, Indian Ocean, and Pacific Ocean and some rivers and lakes

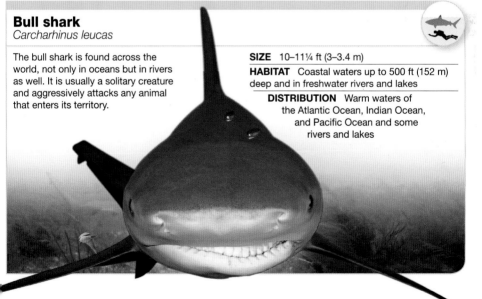

Great hammerhead
Sphyrna mokarran

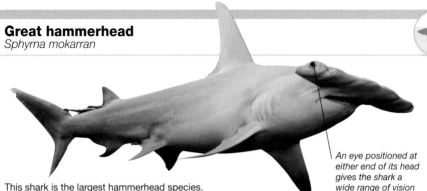

An eye positioned at either end of its head gives the shark a wide range of vision

This shark is the largest hammerhead species. The strange shape of its head helps the great hammerhead find buried stingrays, its favorite prey. Swinging its head from side to side, this shark uses its electrical sense to locate the stingray, pins the ray down with its head, twists the ray around, and bites.

SIZE Up to 20 ft (6.1 m)

HABITAT Coastal, offshore, and oceanic waters up to 262 ft (80 m) deep

DISTRIBUTION Tropical waters of the Atlantic Ocean, Indian Ocean, and Pacific Ocean

Scalloped hammerhead
Sphyrna lewini

ENDANGERED

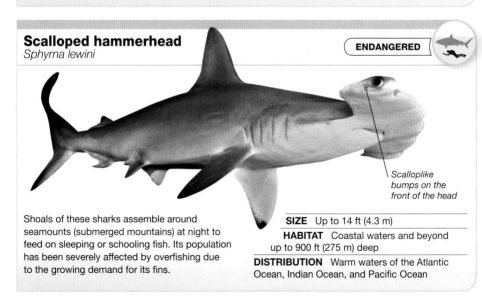

Scalloplike bumps on the front of the head

Shoals of these sharks assemble around seamounts (submerged mountains) at night to feed on sleeping or schooling fish. Its population has been severely affected by overfishing due to the growing demand for its fins.

SIZE Up to 14 ft (4.3 m)

HABITAT Coastal waters and beyond up to 900 ft (275 m) deep

DISTRIBUTION Warm waters of the Atlantic Ocean, Indian Ocean, and Pacific Ocean

Bonnethead shark
Sphyrna tiburo

The head of a bonnethead shark is shaped more like a shovel than a hammer. This allows it to dig out crabs and shellfish.

SIZE Up to 5 ft (1.5 m)

HABITAT Coastal waters up to 262 ft (80 m) deep

DISTRIBUTION Western Atlantic Ocean and eastern Pacific Ocean

Winghead shark
Eusphyra blochii

Long and narrow head blades, known as cephalofoils, give this shark a unique appearance. It feeds on fish, crustaceans, octopuses, and squid.

SIZE Up to 6 ft (1.8 m)

HABITAT Shallow, coastal waters

DISTRIBUTION Northern and eastern Indian Ocean and western Pacific Ocean

Smooth hammerhead
Sphyrna zygaena

The third-largest hammerhead species, the smooth hammerhead is a fearsome predator. It feeds on bony fish, rays, sharks, and squid. It is actively hunted for its fins, which are used to make shark fin soup.

SIZE Up to 13 ft (4 m)

HABITAT Coastal and offshore waters up to at least 66 ft (20 m) deep

DISTRIBUTION Temperate to warm waters of the Atlantic Ocean, Indian Ocean, and Pacific Ocean

Scalloped hammerheads can form schools of up to 500 sharks

SCALLOPED HAMMERHEAD

Unlike most shark species, scalloped hammerheads form schools, often near seamounts, where there is a good supply of food. The largest females swim in the center of a school, which is where males head to find a mate. Males prefer larger females because they produce more pups than smaller females.

Rays, skates, and chimaeras

Like their shark relatives, rays, skates, sawfish, and chimaeras are cartilaginous fish. Rays and skates have flat bodies, with broad winglike fins. Some of them, such as the stingray (left), have sharp stings on their tails, which are used for defense. One family of rays, the sawfish, use their heads rather than their tails for defense. Their long snouts are edged with sharp, toothlike denticles that are ideal for slashing prey as well as defending against attackers.

CHIMAERAS
Found in deep water, chimaeras are also known as rabbitfish because their front cutting teeth and back grinding teeth resemble those of a rabbit.

Shark relatives

Skates, rays, and sawfish can be grouped together in one superorder called Batoidea, with more than 600 species divided into six orders. These fish are close relatives of sharks and share many features with them, including a skeleton made of cartilage. The final group of cartilaginous fish is the chimaeras, which are more distantly related to sharks and skates.

Eye protudes from head

Spiracle used to draw in water, which is then pumped through the gills

Flattened **pectoral fin**

Skates and rays

Skates and rays have a flattened body, with only the eyes and the spiracles—organs used for breathing—on the top. The gills, nostrils, and mouth are underneath. Many skates and rays look like angel sharks, but unlike the sharks their pectoral fins are fused to the body, creating a flattened diamond or circular shape.

Top view of thornback ray

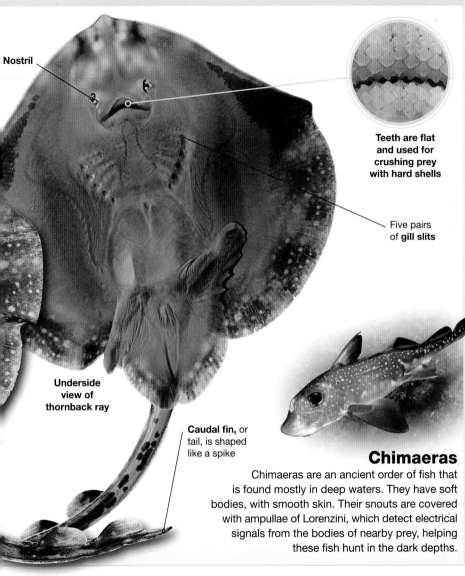

Nostril

Teeth are flat
and used for
crushing prey
with hard shells

Five pairs
of **gill slits**

**Underside
view of
thornback ray**

Caudal fin, or
tail, is shaped
like a spike

Chimaeras

Chimaeras are an ancient order of fish that
is found mostly in deep waters. They have soft
bodies, with smooth skin. Their snouts are covered
with ampullae of Lorenzini, which detect electrical
signals from the bodies of nearby prey, helping
these fish hunt in the dark depths.

A number of features distinguish sawfish from sawsharks.

▲ Sawfish have gills on the underside of the body, while sawsharks have gills on the sides.

▲ The mouth of a sawfish is on the underside of its body. In a sawshark, it is more toward the front of its head.

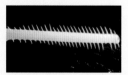

▲ Both sawsharks and sawfish have teeth on each side of the snout, but in sawsharks the teeth are more uneven in length.

Sawfish

Sawfish resemble sawsharks, but are much bigger in size and do not have barbels. All species are endangered—they are slow to reproduce and they get easily entangled in fishing nets.

Largetooth sawfish
Pristis microdon   ENDANGERED

The long denticles on its snout give the largetooth sawfish its name. Despite its fearsome appearance, the fish does not attack humans unless provoked or taken by surprise. This shark is being overfished for its meat and so its populations are under threat.

SIZE 16½–23 ft (5–7 m)

HABITAT Rivers, freshwater lakes, and coastal waters up to 33 ft (10 m) deep

DISTRIBUTION Rivers and lakes of southeastern Asia, Australia, and southeastern Africa and nearby coastal waters

Narrowsnout sawfish
Pristis zijsron

ENDANGERED

This species is the largest of all the sawfish. Like all sawfish, this species keeps its body flat on the seabed but holds its snout upward at an angle while resting. It sleeps during the day and hunts at night, stunning its prey with a sideways swipe of the snout.

SIZE 24 ft (7.3 m)

HABITAT Rivers, freshwater lakes, and coastal waters up to 131 ft (40 m) deep

DISTRIBUTION Indian Ocean, western Pacific Ocean, and rivers and lakes in South Africa and northern New Zealand

Knifetooth sawfish
Anoxypristis cuspidata

ENDANGERED

All teeth are of the same length

The knifetooth sawfish has a narrow snout with 18–22 pairs of daggerlike teeth on it. The skin of the juveniles is smooth, but adults grow thornlike scales on their skin. Like other sawfish, when caught it is known to thrash violently, and it may injure fishermen.

SIZE 15½ ft (4.7 m)

HABITAT Rivers, freshwater lakes, and coastal waters up to 131 ft (40 m) deep

DISTRIBUTION Indian Ocean and western Pacific Ocean

Guitarfish

About 50 species of guitarfish have been identified, and they belong in two orders: Rhinobatiformes and Rhiniformes. These creatures have raylike fins, but their hind body is narrower like a shark.

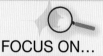
Thornback guitarfish
Platyrhinoidis triseriata

This guitarfish has three parallel rows of large, hooked thorns that run from the middle of its back to its tail. Like sharks and other rays, guitarfish have ampullae of Lorenzini on their snouts, which help them detect electrical signals produced by prey.

SIZE	14½–35 in (37–90 cm)
HABITAT	Coastal waters up to 450 ft (137 m) deep
DISTRIBUTION	Eastern Pacific Ocean

Atlantic guitarfish
Rhinobatos lentiginosus

Also known as the freckled guitarfish, the Atlantic guitarfish is the smallest member of its order. The upper part of its body is covered with freckles while its belly is a pale yellow.

SIZE	Up to 30 in (76 cm)
HABITAT	Coastal waters up to 98 ft (30 m) deep
DISTRIBUTION	Western Atlantic Ocean

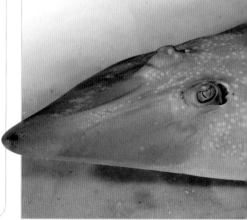

▲ These fish have a triangular body shape, with a pointed snout, broad pectoral fins, and a long tapering tail end.

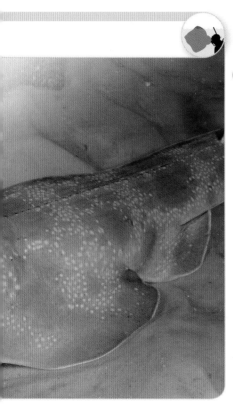

Common guitarfish
Rhinobatos rhinobatos

This fish hunts its prey either by swimming slowly along the bottom of the seabed or lying partially buried in sand and ambushing prey. The common guitarfish feeds on shrimp, crabs, and small fish.

SIZE 2½–5½ ft (0.75–1.7 m)

HABITAT Coastal waters up to 590 ft (180 m) deep

DISTRIBUTION Eastern Atlantic Ocean, Mediterranean Sea, and Black Sea

Skates

Skates are a particular kind of ray that have a kite-shaped, flattened body and winglike pectoral fins. They belong to the order Rajiformes. There are more than 200 species of skate, but many of them are at risk of becoming endangered due to overfishing for their meat and the destruction of their habitats.

Big skate
Raja binoculata

This fish is the largest skate in North America. Raised, pointed denticles (or thorns) are present on the upper surface of the adult's body, while the young have a smoother skin. This skate usually lies hidden in the sand, with only its eyes exposed.

SIZE	3¼–8 ft (1–2.4 m)
HABITAT	Continental shelves up to 656 ft (200 m) deep
DISTRIBUTION	Northeastern Pacific Ocean

Thornback skate
Raja clavata

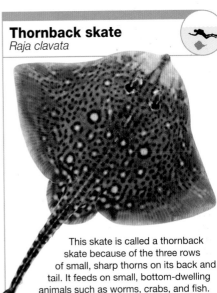

This skate is called a thornback skate because of the three rows of small, sharp thorns on its back and tail. It feeds on small, bottom-dwelling animals such as worms, crabs, and fish.

SIZE	3¼–4¼ ft (1–1.3 m)
HABITAT	Coastal reefs up to 984 ft (300 m) deep
DISTRIBUTION	Northern and eastern Atlantic Ocean, Mediterranean Sea, and Black Sea

Undulate ray
Raja undulata

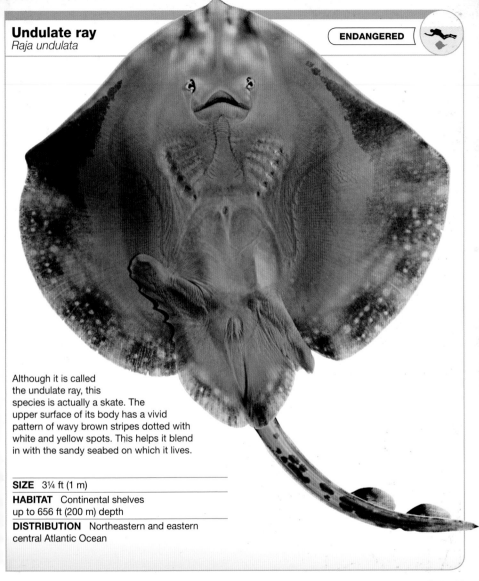

Although it is called
the undulate ray, this
species is actually a skate. The
upper surface of its body has a vivid
pattern of wavy brown stripes dotted with
white and yellow spots. This helps it blend
in with the sandy seabed on which it lives.

SIZE 3¼ ft (1 m)

HABITAT Continental shelves
up to 656 ft (200 m) depth

DISTRIBUTION Northeastern and eastern
central Atlantic Ocean

Common skate ENDANGERED
Dipturus batis

The common skate is the largest skate species. It feeds on bottom-dwelling crustaceans, shellfish, and fish. This skate envelops its prey in its pectoral fins before capturing and eating it.

SIZE 3¼–9½ ft (1–2.9 m)

HABITAT Coastal waters up to 1,970 ft (600 m) deep

DISTRIBUTION Northeastern and eastern Atlantic Ocean

Thornback skate
Dentiraja lemprieri

The thornback skate is a slow swimmer and often lies motionless on the seabed. It feeds on crabs, shrimp, lobsters, and other small, bottom-dwelling animals, including fish. The female thornback skate is larger than the male and lays dozens of eggs in a season.

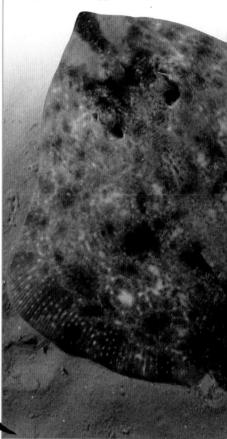

Thorny skate
Amblyraja radiata

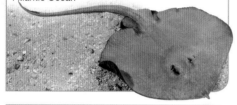

This skate has a very rough upper body surface, with small thorns scattered all over its disc and tail. The thorny skate also has a distinct black spot on the tip of its tail.

SIZE Up to 3½ ft (1.05 m)

HABITAT Continental shelves and beyond up to 3,280 ft (1,000 m) deep

DISTRIBUTION Northeastern and northwestern Atlantic Ocean

SIZE 21½ in (55 cm)

HABITAT Continental shelves up to 558 ft (170 m) deep

DISTRIBUTION Southwestern Pacific Ocean and eastern Indian Ocean, around Tasmania

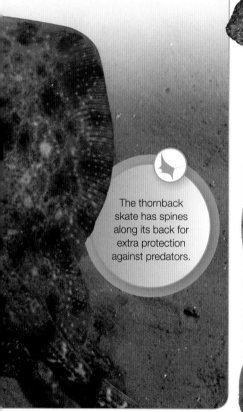

The thornback skate has spines along its back for extra protection against predators.

Peacock skate
Pavoraja nitida

The peacock skate has a prominent black patch on the lower side of its snout tip. The young skates can often be seen following their mother.

SIZE Up to 14½ in (37 cm)

HABITAT Continental shelves and beyond up to 1,280 ft (390 m) deep

DISTRIBUTION Southwestern Pacific Ocean and eastern Indian Ocean

Little skate
Leucoraja erinacea

The little skate is more active at night and in dark conditions. Its tail contains an electric organ, which is thought to help it communicate with other skates and detect potential mates.

SIZE Up to 21¼ in (54 cm)

HABITAT Continental shelves and beyond, up to 1,080 ft (329 m) deep

DISTRIBUTION Northwestern Atlantic Ocean

Electric rays

Electric rays have special organs in their bodies that produce an electrical current, which can reach 220 volts in the largest species. They use this both to stun prey and in defense. The best-known member of this family is the torpedo ray, which inspired the name of the torpedo weapon.

Giant electric ray
Narcine entemedor

The giant electric ray, also known as the Cortez electric ray, feeds at night and spends the day lying half-buried in sand. While searching for food, it glides along the seabed using its flexible fins.

SIZE Up to 36½ in (93 cm)

HABITAT Sandy seabeds up to 328 ft (100 m) deep

DISTRIBUTION Eastern and southeastern Pacific Ocean

Ocellated electric ray
Diplobatis ommata

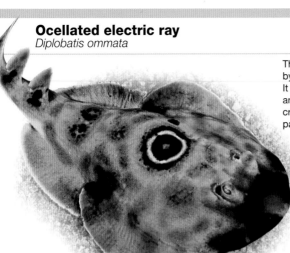

This electric ray is easily recognized by the bulls-eye pattern on its back. It feeds on small fish, crabs, shrimp, and small worms. This solitary creature is capable of generating a painful electric shock in self defense.

SIZE Up to 10 in (25 cm)

HABITAT Rocky reefs up to 308 ft (94 m) deep

DISTRIBUTION Eastern Pacific Ocean

Marbled electric ray
Torpedo marmorata

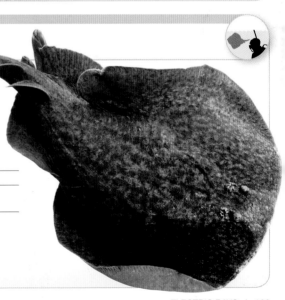

The marbled electric ray, or spotted electric ray, is a slow-moving predator that attacks its prey from below, capturing its victims after stunning them with strong electric shocks.

SIZE 8½–24 in (21–61 cm)

HABITAT Sandy, stony, or rocky seabeds up to 328 ft (100 m) deep

DISTRIBUTION Eastern Atlantic Ocean and Mediterranean Sea

Common torpedo
Torpedo torpedo

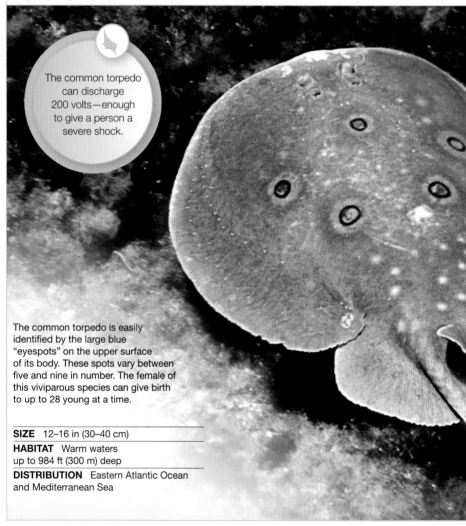

The common torpedo can discharge 200 volts—enough to give a person a severe shock.

The common torpedo is easily identified by the large blue "eyespots" on the upper surface of its body. These spots vary between five and nine in number. The female of this viviparous species can give birth to up to 28 young at a time.

SIZE 12–16 in (30–40 cm)

HABITAT Warm waters up to 984 ft (300 m) deep

DISTRIBUTION Eastern Atlantic Ocean and Mediterranean Sea

Black-spotted torpedo
Torpedo fuscomaculata

A lesser-known ray, this torpedo is confined mostly to the waters near southern Africa. It feeds on cuttlefish and a variety of small fish, including sea bream and beaked sandfish.

SIZE   Up to 25 in (64 cm)

HABITAT   Continental shelves and beyond, up to 1,440 ft (439 m) deep

DISTRIBUTION   Southeastern Atlantic Ocean and western Indian Ocean

Stingrays

Stingrays belong to the order Myliobatiformes. Their popular name comes from the one or more venomous stings on their tail. However, not all stingrays have stings. Most do, including the four whiptail stingrays on these pages, but butterfly rays and manta rays do not.

Common stingray
Dasyatis pastinaca

Humans have been familiar with the common stingray since ancient times. The venom in its sting was once considered to have no cure and even turn iron to rust. However, although its sting can cause a very painful wound, it is not usually fatal to humans.

Leopard stingray
Himantura uarnak

Also called the reticulate whipray, this fish gets its name from the pattern on the upper surface of its body, which resembles a leopard's skin. This species hunts at night and spends most of the daytime lying still on the seabed.

SIZE   1–8¼ ft (0.3–2.5 m)

HABITAT   Continental shelves up to 656 ft (200 m) deep

DISTRIBUTION   Northeastern Atlantic Ocean, Mediterranean Sea, and Black Sea

SIZE   Up to 6½ ft (2 m)

HABITAT   Seabeds up to 164 ft (50 m) deep

DISTRIBUTION   Indian Ocean and western Pacific Ocean

FOCUS ON...
TAIL
Species in the family of whiptail stingrays have a tail that is longer than the body.

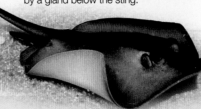

▼ A whiptail's main defense is its tail. It has up to three stings, which are used to inject predators with venom produced by a gland below the sting.

Bluespotted ray
Taeniura lymma

This stingray spends most of its time near rocky and coral reefs. However, when the water level rises during high tide, it moves into shallow lagoons. It feeds on shrimp, small fish, crabs, and worms.

SIZE 28–35 in (70–90 cm)

HABITAT Coral and rocky reefs and nearby sandflats, up to 82 ft (25 m) deep

DISTRIBUTION Indian Ocean and western Pacific Ocean

Southern stingray
Dasyatis americana

This stingray finds its food by flapping its fins over the seabed to expose crabs and other crustaceans hidden beneath. This docile creature uses its long, barbed whiplike tail only in defense.

SIZE Up to 8¼ ft (2.5 m)

HABITAT Seabeds up to 174 ft (53 m) deep

DISTRIBUTION Western Atlantic Ocean, Gulf of Mexico, and Caribbean Sea

Cowtail stingray
Pastinachus sephen

This fish can easily be recognized by the large flaglike fold on its tail. The cowtail stingray is threatened from overfishing because its skin is used to make shagreen, a high-quality leather.

SIZE 4½–10 ft (1.4–3 m)

HABITAT Coral reefs, rocky or sandy seabeds, and rivers up to 197 ft (60 m) deep

DISTRIBUTION Indian Ocean and western Pacific Ocean

Round stingray
Urobatis halleri

As in some other stingray species, the main spine on the tail of the round stingray is periodically shed. Early in the year, round stingrays have one spine on the tail. By summer, a second spine grows. By winter, the original spine falls off and the second spine replaces it. These stingrays are found in warm waters above 50°F (10°C).

SIZE Up to 18 in (45 cm)

HABITAT Muddy or sandy seabeds up to 298 ft (91 m) deep

DISTRIBUTION Eastern Pacific Ocean

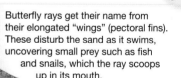

Spiny butterfly ray
Gymnura altavela

Butterfly rays get their name from their elongated "wings" (pectoral fins). These disturb the sand as it swims, uncovering small prey such as fish and snails, which the ray scoops up in its mouth.

SIZE 6½–10 ft (2–3 m)

HABITAT Sandy seabeds up to 180 ft (55 m) deep

DISTRIBUTION Western and eastern Atlantic Ocean and Mediterranean Sea

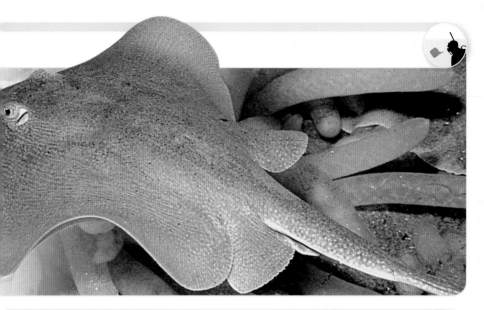

Ocellate stingray
Potamotrygon motoro

The ocellate stingray is also known as the peacock-eye stingray because of the orange spots on its back. Newborn rays prey on plankton, but as they grow up, they start feeding on mollusks, crustaceans, and the larvae of water insects.

SIZE Up to 35 in (90 cm)

HABITAT Freshwater

DISTRIBUTION
Several rivers in
South America

*Eye raised
above body surface*

Spotted eagle ray
Aetobatus narinari

The spotted eagle ray swims by beating its pectoral fins in a similar way to a bird flapping its wings. In open waters, these fish often form large schools and swim close to the surface. Its attractive dorsal spots make it a favorite at public aquariums.

SIZE 3¼–13 ft (1–4 m)

HABITAT Continental shelves up to 197 ft (60 m) deep

DISTRIBUTION Western and eastern Atlantic Ocean, Indian Ocean, and western, central, and eastern Pacific Ocean

The spotted eagle ray can leap clear out of the water to escape predators.

Giant manta ray
Manta birostris

A filter feeder, the giant manta ray feeds by pulling in water through its mouth and passing the water through its gills. Special organs on its gills, called gill rakers, strain the plankton out of the water. An average-sized manta eats up to 66 lb (30 kg) of plankton in a single day.

SIZE   14¾–30 ft (4.5–9 m)

HABITAT   Near coral and rocky reefs up to 390 ft (120 m) deep

DISTRIBUTION   Atlantic Ocean, Pacific Ocean, and Indian Ocean

Javanese cownose ray
Rhinoptera javanica

This unusual-looking ray has an indented forehead and a double-lobed snout, which looks like a flap. It has a kite-shaped body, which is brown on top and white below. Its long tail is armed with one or more stings.

SIZE   3¼–5 ft (1–1.5 m)

HABITAT   Coastal waters up to 98 ft (30 m) deep

DISTRIBUTION   Indian Ocean and western Pacific Ocean

MANTA RAY
Manta rays are sometimes called devil rays because of the "horns" projecting from their heads. When they feed, they unfurl these fleshy lobes, which direct water into the mouth. They strain out plankton from the water using spongy tissue in their gills.

The largest species of ray, the giant manta ray can grow up to **30 ft (9 m)** across from the tip of one fin to the other

Chimaeras

Although chimaeras and sharks share a common ancestor, the chimaeras began evolving separately from the sharks around 400 million years ago. These fish have a large head and their teeth are arranged like those in a rabbit's mouth, with teeth for grabbing and slicing at the front and teeth for grinding at the back.

Spotted ratfish
Hydrolagus colliei

The spotted ratfish is so named because its tail resembles that of a rat. The dorsal fin of this fish has a venomous spine, which is used in defense. A strong sense of smell allows it to locate prey easily, such as crabs, clams, and small fish.

SIZE 23½ in (60 cm)

HABITAT Coastal waters and continental slopes up to 2,950 ft (900 m) deep

DISTRIBUTION Northeastern and eastern Pacific Ocean

Spine on dorsal fin

Knifenose chimaera
Rhinochimaera pacifica

Also known as the Pacific spookfish, this chimaera is named for its long, conical snout. The snout is covered with sensory pores that help it detect prey, most likely through a combination of smell and vibration.

SIZE Up to 4¼ ft (1.3 m)

HABITAT Offshore up to 4,265 ft (1,300 m) deep

DISTRIBUTION Western, southwestern, and southeastern Pacific Ocean and eastern Indian Ocean

Elephant fish
Callorhinchus milii

This chimaera has a long, fleshy snout that resembles an elephant's trunk; it uses its snout to sense and unearth shellfish from muddy seabeds. It also has a spine in front of its dorsal fin that it uses to defend itself against predators.

SIZE 2½–4 ft (0.75–1.25 m)

HABITAT Continental shelves up to 745 ft (227 m) deep

DISTRIBUTION Southwestern Pacific Ocean

...ting facts

...ust move left or right to avoid collisions. They also cannot swim backward.

- **The fastest-moving shark** is the shortfin mako shark. It can reach speeds of more than 35 mph (56 kph).

- **Some large species of shark undergo long migrations.** Atlantic blue sharks may do a round trip of up to 10,500 miles (17,000 km) in about 14 months, traveling between feeding grounds and breeding areas.

- **A great hammerhead shark** was recently tracked covering 745 miles (1,200 km) in 62 days.

- **Bull sharks** are the only common sharks that migrate from the salty oceans to rivers, traveling upstream to find food.

- **Perhaps the least enthusiastic traveler** is the nurse shark. It remains in an area of a few dozen square miles for its entire life.

In some sharks, the first embryo to develop eats the other embryos while still inside the mother. This is called oophagy.

LIFE CYCLE

▶ **Lemon sharks** can give birth to up to 17 pups in one litter.

▶ **Great hammerhead sharks** can give birth to up to 40 pups at once.

▶ **Whale sharks** can carry up to 300 embryos at a time. However, not all of these embryos hatch into pups.

▶ **Female sandbar sharks** start breeding when about 13 years old, but then only produce a few pups every two years.

▶ **Most sharks** live for 20 to 30 years, but some reach 80. Experts suspect that the large, slow whale shark may be capable of surviving for well over 100 years, making it one of the longest-living animals on the Earth.

▶ **Some deep-sea sharks** do not mature until they are at least 40 years old.

▶ **The liver** of a basking shark becomes even larger during pregnancy. This happens because the liver acts as a storehouse for energy that the shark needs during its three-year-long pregnancy.

HUNTING AND FEEDING

♦ **A shark's ears** are sensitive enough to pick up sounds from several hundred yards away, helping it find prey easily.

♦ **Sharks have powerful jaws** and some sharks are capable of exerting 132 lb (60 kg) of pressure per tooth when they bite.

♦ **Great white sharks** may not eat for several days after a heavy meal.

♦ **Sharks living in cold water** can heat their eyes using a special organ next to a muscle in their eye socket. This lets them hunt in extreme temperatures.

♦ **Many sharks have a keen sense of smell** so powerful that they can detect a single drop of blood in a bathtub of water.

DANGER

★ **Great white sharks** may be responsible for more attacks on people than any other species of shark. However, tiger and bull sharks also top the list of sharks that are known to attack humans.

★ **Second Beach** near Port St. John's, South Africa, may be the world's most dangerous beach. From 2007 to 2012, at least one person a year was killed by a shark.

★ **Several dozen shark attacks** on humans are reported every year, while perhaps 100 million sharks are killed by humans each year.

★ **Aside from humans,** a shark's biggest enemy is another shark—many sharks are known to prey on members of their own or other shark species.

RAYS AND RELATIVES

▶ **The green sawfish and giant manta ray** are the biggest members of the superorder Batoidea, growing to more than 24 ft (7.3 m) long.

▶ **The giant manta ray** is also the widest member of the ray family—it can reach up to 30 ft (9 m).

▶ **The knifetooth sawfish** can give birth to up to 23 young.

Some manta rays leap out of the water apparently for fun, jumping forward and landing headfirst or tailfirst and even doing backflips.

▶ The wound caused by a **stingray's venom** can take more than a year to heal.

▶ **The venom** from the spine of a stingray was used by ancient Greek dentists as an anesthetic.

Largest and smallest sharks

THE LARGEST

Sharks include the largest fish in the world. They are among the oceans' top predators, feeding on fish, crustaceans, seals, and even dolphins and whales. Here are some of the longest sharks and their recorded lengths.

⑩ Bigeye thresher shark
This shark grows to a maximum length of 15 ft (4.6 m), with its tail accounting for about half of this length.

⑨ Bluntnose sixgill shark or cow shark
The largest member of its family, this shark reaches a maximum length of 15¾ ft (4.8 m).

⑧ Thresher shark
Measured from the tip of the snout to the end of its tail, the thresher shark has a top length of 20 ft (6 m).

⑦ Great hammerhead shark
The largest of all hammerhead species, the great hammerhead shark has been known to reach a length of 20 ft (6 m).

⑥ Great white shark
Some female great whites can reach 21 ft (6.4 m). They are stockier and heavier than the tiger sharks, although they are about the same size.

⑤ Tiger shark
The largest tiger sharks can grow to at least 21½ ft (6.5 m) long.

④ Pacific sleeper shark
This shark has a maximum recorded length of 23 ft (7 m).

③ Greenland shark
A close relative of the Pacific sleeper shark, the Greenland shark can grow to a length of 24 ft (7.3 m).

② Basking shark
The basking shark reaches a maximum length of 40½ ft (12.3 m).

The two largest sharks in the world—the basking shark and whale shark—feed on tiny animal plankton.

① Whale shark
The whale shark is the largest shark in the world. The largest official record is 45 ft (13.7 m), but other reports claim lengths of up to 59 ft (18 m).

THE SMALLEST

These are some of the smallest sharks and their maximum recorded adult lengths. Many small sharks live deep in the ocean and are rarely seen. Figuring out to what length a species grows is often based on just one or two individuals that have been caught accidentally.

⑩ Shorttail lantern shark

Living at depths of up to 1,575 ft (480 m), the shorttail lantern shark has a recorded maximum length of only 16½ in (42 cm).

⑨ Longnose pygmy shark

The rare longnose pygmy shark reaches a length of 14½ in (37 cm).

⑧ Granular dogfish

The granular dogfish has been found in two regions near South America—the Falkland Islands and Chile. It grows to just over 11 in (28 cm).

⑦ Spined pygmy catshark

Female spined pygmy catsharks reach a length of 11 in (28 cm).

⑥ Thorny lantern shark

As in most shark species, the female matures at a larger size than the male. She reaches up to 10½ in (27 cm) long.

⑤ Pygmy shark

The pygmy shark grows to just 10½ in (27 cm) long.

④ Green lantern shark

The green lantern shark reaches a maximum length of 10 in (26 cm).

Sharks continue to grow throughout their lives, although the rate of growth slows down as they get older.

③ African lantern shark

This lantern shark can reach 9½ in (24 cm) in length. It lives in the dark zone, some 3,280 ft (1,000 m) below the surface of the sea.

② Broadnose catshark

Only one broadnose catshark has ever been caught. It measured 9½ in (24 cm) long.

① Dwarf lantern shark

Measuring up to 8½ in (21 cm) in length, the dwarf lantern shark is probably the world's smallest shark.

GLOSSARY

Adaptation An evolutionary process that enables living things to fit their environment as well as possible.

Ampullae of Lorenzini Tiny sensors on the snout of a shark or a ray that help it pick up electrical signals from prey. Sharks and rays possibly use these sensors to sense the Earth's magnetic field to help find their way.

Anal fin A fin located on the underside of the body in some sharks.

Anatomy The body structure of a life-form or any of its parts.

Barbel A slender, whiskerlike organ, or feeler, found near the mouth of some sharks. It is used to search the seabed for food.

Buoyancy The ability or tendency of an object or organism to float. Sharks have oil-filled livers to help their buoyancy.

Bycatch Sharks and other sea creatures that by chance get caught on baited lines or in fishing nets set for other fish.

Camouflage Colors or patterns that help an animal to blend in with its surroundings.

Carnivore An animal that eats only meat.

Cartilage A hard yet flexible tissue that forms the skeleton of cartilaginous fish. It is lighter and more flexible than bone.

Cartilaginous fish Fish that have skeletons made of cartilage rather than bone. They include sharks, skates, rays, and chimaeras.

Cavity A hollow area within an object or an organism.

Caudal fin The shark's tail. Sharks have caudal fins of many different shapes and sizes.

Conservation The process of protecting or preserving of animals and their habitats.

Continental shelf The part of the edge of a continent partially submerged in relatively shallow waters.

Continental slope A steep slope from a continental shelf to the ocean floor.

Crustacean A type of invertebrate with jointed legs. Crustaceans usually have hard outer shells. Copepods, krill, and crabs are examples of crustaceans.

Denticles Scales that cover a shark's skin. They are toothlike and dense and unlike those on bony fish. Denticles are made from the same minerals as teeth. They have different shapes depending on where they are on the shark's body. The ones on the snout are rounded, while those on the back are pointed.

Dorsal fin A large fin in the middle of a shark's back that prevents it from rolling over. Some sharks also have a second, smaller dorsal fin near the tail.

Embryo An unborn animal that is developing inside its mother's womb or in an egg.

Enamel The outer coating of teeth. Enamel is the hardest substance in an animal's body.

Endangered species A species that is in danger of becoming extinct. Critically endangered species (such as Ganges sharks) are in immediate danger of dying out if existing conditions do not change.

Evolution The gradual change in living organisms that occurs over many generations.

Extinct A species that has died out. *Megalodon* sharks are extinct.

Feeler An organ, such as a tentacle or barbel, in some animals that helps them to touch or sense.

Filter feeder An animal that feeds by taking in large amounts of water that contains particles of food such as plankton, which are then strained out of the water.

Finning Chopping fins off sharks to sell them. Often, the animal is thrown back into the sea, where it drowns, since it can no longer swim.

Fossil The remains of an ancient animal or plant, preserved in rock.

Gestation The period between conception and birth in which a growing embryo is carried in the womb of the mother.

Gills Feathery structures in a shark's throat region that extract oxygen from the water that is needed to help provide energy.

Gill rakers Projections like the teeth of a comb found in the gills of some fish, including sharks.

They strain tiny organisms from the water that flows over the gills.

Gill slit An opening in the shark's skin from which water flows out. Most sharks have five gill slits.

Habitat The environment in which an animal (or any life-form) lives.

Invertebrate An animal without a backbone.

Lateral line A line of cells along the sides of a shark that are sensitive to changes in water pressure and can detect movement in the water. This is useful for the shark in dark or murky waters.

Migration The process of moving from one place to another according to the seasons, usually to find food or to breed.

Nictitating membrane A special eyelid found in some animals and birds that is translucent or transparent and helps to protect the eye or to keep it moist.

Nocturnal An animal that is active at night.

Oviparous Producing eggs that hatch outside the mother's body.

Ovoviviparous Producing eggs that hatch inside the mother's body.

Oxygen A gas that is found in air and water. Almost all living things need oxygen to survive.

Pectoral fin One of a pair of fins located under the front of a shark's body. The fish uses these to steer and generate lift in the water. They also act as brakes when necessary.

Pelagic Related to or living in the open ocean.

Pelvic fin One of a pair of fins located under the rear of a shark's body. These work with other fins to control swimming.

Plankton The mass of tiny plants and animals that float around in the ocean and are eaten by many larger animals.

Predator An animal that hunts, kills, or eats other animals.

Prey An animal that is hunted, killed, or eaten by a predator.

Pup A baby shark.

Pupping ground An area where sharks gather to give birth.

Regurgitation The process in which an animal releases undigested food from its mouth.

Scavenger An animal that searches for food scraps, rather than hunting prey. Scavengers often eat the remains of animals killed by predators.

School A large group of fish swimming close together and moving as one. Also called a shoal.

Seamount An underwater mountain or volcano.

Shagreen The rough skin of many sharks and rays.

Snout The front part of a shark's head.

Species A group of plants or animals that share features and can breed only with one another.

Spiracles An extra pair of gill openings that supply oxygen to a shark's eyes and brain. Rays also use spiracles to pump water over their gills while they are resting on the seabed.

Streamlined A smooth shape that is less resistant to air or water. Having a streamlined body helps a shark to swim faster.

Tagging A method of tracking and studying sharks in the wild, often by attaching computerized tags to their fins so their movements can be detected and recorded via a satellite.

Tapetum A layer of cells at the back of a shark's eye that reflects light, helping the fish to see clearly in the dark.

Temperate Mild weather or climate.

Tendril A slender armlike structure found in certain organisms. It is used to clasp prey or to move.

Tropical Hot and humid climate or weather as in the tropics.

Vertebrate An animal that has a backbone.

Vertical migration Movement of marine creatures from deep to shallow water or vice versa. Planktonic organisms migrate in this way daily, and they are often followed by sharks and other predators.

Viviparous Producing young that remain in the mother's body until they are fully formed and ready to be born.

Zoology The branch of science that deals with animals and animal life.

Index

Acknowledgments

Dorling Kindersley would like to thank:
Monica Byles for proofreading; Helen Peters
for indexing; David Roberts and Rob Campbell
for database creation; Claire Bowers, Fabian
Harry, Romaine Werblow, and Rose Horridge
for DK Picture Library assistance; Ritu Mishra
for editorial assistance; and Isha Nagar for
design assistance.

The publishers would also like to thank the
following for their kind permission to reproduce
their photographs:

(Key: a-above; b-below/bottom; c-center; f-far;
l-left; r-right; t-top)

1 FLPA: ImageBroker (c). 2–3 Corbis: Denis
Scott (crb). 4–5 Getty Images: Fleetham Dave /
Perspectives (c). 6 marinethemes.com: Kelvin
Aitken (tl); Andy Murch (bl). 7 marinethemes.
com: Kelvin Aitken (cr). 8 Dorling Kindersley:
Natural History Museum, London (c).
marinethemes.com: Kelvin Aitken (bl, bc); Saul
Gonor (cl). 8–9 Dorling Kindersley: Natural
History Museum, London (c). 9 Corbis: Jeffrey L.
Rotman (tr). Dorling Kindersley: Natural History
Museum, London (bl). marinethemes.com:
Kelvin Aitken (br); Andy Murch (cl); Franco Banfi
(bl). 10 marinethemes.com: Kelvin Aitken (b).
11 marinethemes.com: Kelvin Aitken (tr, crb,
br). 12 Corbis: Douglas P. Wilson / Frank Lane
Picture Agency (cl, clb, bl). 13 Corbis: Jeffrey L.
Rotman (r). SeaPics.com: Doug Perrine (b). 14
Alamy Images: Dan Callister (b). marinethemes.
com: Kelvin Aitken (a). 15 Corbis: Tom
Brakefield (tr). Getty Images: James Forte /
National Geographic (b); Jeff Rotman / Iconica
(tc). marinethemes.com: Kelvin Aitken (cb).
16–17 Corbis: Clouds Hill Imaging Ltd.. 18 Getty
Images: Barcroft Media (br); Jonathan S. Blair /
National Geographic (b). marinethemes.com:
Kelvin Aitken (cr). 21 Getty Images: Stephen
Frink / The Image Bank (t). marinethemes.com:
Kelvin Aitken (tc). SeaPics.com: Doug Perrine
(tc). 22 Alamy Images: Mark Conlin (b). Dorling
Kindersley: The Trustees of the British Museum
(c). 22–23 Getty Images: Yoshikazu Tsuno / Afp
(b). 23 SeaPics.com: Doug Perrine (tr). 24
Dorling Kindersley: Natural History Museum,
London (c). 26–27 Science Photo Library:
Christian Darkin. 28 Corbis: Tim Davis. 29
marinethemes.com: Andy Murch (bc). 30 Alamy
Images: Mark Conlin (bc). marinethemes.com:
Saul Gonor (bl); Andy Murch (crb). SeaPics.com:
Marty Snyderman (cl). 31 marinethemes.com:
Kelvin Aitken (cl, bc, c, tl). Oceanwidelmages.
com: Bill Boyle (br). 32 marinethemes.com:
Kelvin Aitken (cr, tl, cl, bl). 33 Dorling
Kindersley: Jon Baldur Hliðberg (www.fauna.is)
(cl). marinethemes.com: Kelvin Aitken (tr, br). 34
marinethemes.com: Kelvin Aitken (t). 34–35
marinethemes.com: Andy Murch (b). 35
marinethemes.com: Kelvin Aitken (tr). naturepl.
com: Ian Coleman (WAC) (tl). 36 marinethemes.
com: Kelvin Aitken (t). 37 marinethemes.com:
Kelvin Aitken (tl); Ken Hoppen (br).
Oceanwidelmages.com: Rudie Kuiter (bl).
38 Oceanwidelmages.com: Rudie Kuiter (b).
39 marinethemes.com: Kelvin Aitken (tl).
www.uwp.no: Erling Svenson (b). 40
Oceanwidelmages.com: Rudie Kuiter (tl). 40
marinethemes.com: Kelvin Aitken (b). SeaPics.
com: Stephen Kajiura (tl). 41 marinethemes.

com: Kelvin Aitken (br); (clb). 42 naturepl.com:
Doug Perrine. 43 marinethemes.com: Kelvin
Aitken (t, b). Photolibrary: (bl). 44–45
Oceanwidelmages.com: Rudie Kuiter (r). 46
Photolibrary: (bl). 46–47 Corbis: Norbert Wu /
Science Faction (c). 47 Alamy Images:
WaterFrame (r). 48 SeaPics.com: Kubo /
e-Photography (cl). 48–49 marinethemes.com:
Kelvin Aitken (bc). 49 Oceanwidelmages.com:
Rudie Kuiter (br). SeaPics.com: Marty
Sniderman (tr). 50 marinethemes.com:
Kelvin Aitken (tl, cl, bl); Andy Murch (br).
51 marinethemes.com: Kelvin Aitken (t).
Oceanwidelmages.com: Bill Boyle (b).
52–53 naturepl.com: Alex Mustard. 54–55
Ecoscene: Andy Murch (l). 55 SeaPics.com:
Mark Strickland (br). 56 marinethemes.com:
Mark Conlin (cl). 57 Dorling Kindersley: Natural
History Museum, London (tc). marinethemes.
com: Kelvin Aitken (tl); Mark Conlin (tr).
58 marinethemes.com: Kelvin Aitken (tr).
Oceanwidelmages.com: David Fleetham (br).
SeaPics.com: D. R. Schrichte (tl). 59
marinethemes.com: Kelvin Aitken. 60
marinethemes.com: Kelvin Aitken (tl, bl); Jez
Tryner (cl). Oceanwidelmages.com: Rudie
Kuiter (br). 61 Alamy Images: Andy Murch /
Vwpics (br). Oceanwidelmages.com: Rudie
Kuiter (tr). SeaPics.com: Scott Michael (bl).
62–63 Getty Images: Digital Vision / Justin
Lewis (l). 62 marinethemes.com: Mike Parry
(bl). 63 Alamy Images: Underwater Imaging (r).
64–65 Alamy Images: Martin Strmiska.
66–67 Alamy Images: Reinhard Dirscherl (c).
67 marinethemes.com: Kelvin Aitken / First Light (tr).
68–69 marinethemes.com: Kelvin Aitken.
70. naturepl.com: Doug Perrine (r). 71 Alamy
Images: WaterFrame (b). 72 SeaPics.com: Lisa
Collins (t). 73 SeaPics.com: Scott Michael (b);
D. R. Schrichte (t). 74 marinethemes.com:
Kelvin Aitken (cr); Mary Malloy (cl). 75 Dorling
Kindersley: Natural History Museum, London (tl).
marinethemes.com: Kelvin Aitken (tc); Andy
Murch (tr). NHPA / Photoshot: Franco Banfi (r).
76 SeaPics.com: Stephen Kajiura (tr). 76–77
Ardea: Gavin Parsons (r). 78–79 marinethemes.
com: Saul Gonor. 80–81 marinethemes.com:
Kelvin Aitken (b). 81 Corbis: Jeffrey L. Rotman
(tr). 82–83 Dorling Kindersley: Jeremy Hunt –
modelmaker (c). 82 Alamy Images: Doug Perrine
(tl). 83 marinethemes.com: Andy Murch (tr).
84–85 Alamy Images: Dan Callister. 86 FLPA:
Norbert Wu / Minden Pictures (c). 87
marinethemes.com: Kelvin Aitken (tr, tl); David
Fleetham (tr). SeaPics.com: Peter McMillan (cl);
Scott Michael (c). 88–89 Oceanwidelmages.
com: Rudie Kuiter (c). Photolibrary: (bc).
88 marinethemes.com: Ken Hoppen (cla).
89 naturepl.com: Alex Mustard (br). 90–91
naturepl.com: Florian Graner (tc). 90 SeaPics.
com: Doug Perrine (b). 92 naturepl.com: Doug
Perrine (bl). 92–93 marinethemes.com: Kelvin
Aitken (bc). SeaPics.com: Doug Perrine (bl). 94
93 SeaPics.com: Doug Perrine (bl). 94
marinethemes.com: Andy Murch. 95
marinethemes.com: Kelvin Aitken (b). 96–97
Getty Images: Paul Kay / Oxford Scientific. 98
Alamy Images: Mark Conlin (bl). marinethemes.
com: Kelvin Aitken (tl). 101 marinethemes.com:
Kelvin Aitken (b). 102–103 Science Photo
Library: Jason Isley / Scubazoo (l). 103 Thomas
Gloerfelt: (br). 104–105 Getty Images:

Georgette Douwma / Digital Vision (bc).
marinethemes.com: David Fleetham (tc).
105 Alamy Images: WaterFrame (br). 106–107
Getty Images: Alexander Safonov / Flickr. 108
Dorling Kindersley: David Peart (b). 108–109
marinethemes.com: Andy Murch (c). 109 Getty
Images: Rainer Schimpf / Gallo Images (b). 110
Dorling Kindersley: Rough Guides (tl). Getty
Images: James R. D. Scott / Flickr (bl). 110–111
Alamy Images: Andy Murch / Vwpics (bc). 111
marinethemes.com: Andy Murch (r). 112–113
marinethemes.com: Andy Murch. 114 Getty
Images: Stephen Frink / Stone (tr).
marinethemes.com: David Fleetham (b). 115
marinethemes.com: Stephen Wong (b). 116
Corbis: Norbert Wu / Science Faction (t). Getty
Images: Jonathan Bird / Peter Arnold (b). 117
Corbis: Andy Murch / Visuals Unlimited (bl).
Getty Images: Gerard Soury / Oxford Scientific
(tl). SeaPics.com: Stephen Kajiura (tr). 118–119
SeaPics.com: Martin Strmiska. 120 Corbis: Paul
Souders. 121 marinethemes.com: Kelvin Aitken
(bc). 123 Corbis: Norbert Wu / Science Faction
(crb). marinethemes.com: Kelvin Aitken (tr). 124
marinethemes.com: Kelvin Aitken (cl, br); Andy
Murch (b). 125 FLPA: Norbert Wu / Minden
Pictures (b). marinethemes.com: Andy Murch
(c). 126 Oceanwidelmages.com: Andy Murch
(bl). 126–127 Andy Murch / Elasmodiver.com:
(bc). 127 marinethemes.com: Andy Murch (tc).
Robert Harding Picture Library: Marevision /
age fotostock (cr). 128 Getty Images: Visuals
Unlimited, Inc. / Andy Murch (cl). 130 Getty
Images: Bill Curtsinger / National Geographic
(bl). marinethemes.com: Kelvin Aitken (cl).
130–131 marinethemes.com: Kelvin Aitken (bc).
131 Getty Images: Visuals Unlimited, Inc. / Andy
Murch (tr). marinethemes.com: Kelvin Aitken
(tr). 132 marinethemes.com: Andy Murch (b).
133 marinethemes.com: Andy Murch (b).
134–135 SuperStock: age fotostock (t).
135 SeaPics.com: Manfred Bail (t). 136
marinethemes.com: David Fleetham (cr).
137 Corbis: Stephen Frink (tl). SuperStock:
age fotostock (tr). 138 Getty Images: Visuals
Unlimited, Inc. / Andy Murch (cl, bl). 139
marinethemes.com: Andy Murch (b). SeaPics.
com: Mark Conlin (t). 140 Corbis: Stephen Frink
/ Aurora Photos. 141 Alamy Images: blickwinkel
/ Schmidbauer (b). Getty Images: Roger Munns
- Subazoo / Science Faction (t). 142–143
marinethemes.com: Kelvin Aitken. 144
Oceanwidelmages.com: Andy Murch (b).
145 marinethemes.com: Kelvin Aitken (t, b).

Jacket images: Front: Alamy Images: Masa
Ushioda / Stephen Frink Collection (c); Dorling
Kindersley: Jeremy Hunt - modelmaker (r, cla,
cla / Spinner shark, clb, crb / Great white shark,
crb / Spinner shark, br, Natural History Museum,
London tl, tc, tl / Bramble shark, tr / Gill rakers,
tr / Megalodon, tl, cla / Striatolamia, crb,
cb, fclb, clb/ Great white shark jaw, bl, bc; Back:
Dorling Kindersley: Jeremy Hunt - modelmaker
cla, Natural History Museum, London clb; Spine:
Alamy Images: Masa Ushioda /
Stephen Frink Collection t.

All other images © Dorling Kindersley

For further information see: www.dkimages.com